LEE CANTER'S
ASSERTIVE DISCIPLINE®
FOR PARENTS

Lee Canter's
ASSERTIVE

DISCIPLINE®
for Parents

Lee Canter
with Marlene Canter

CANTER & ASSOCIATES INC.
Distributed by Harper & Row

FIRST EDITION

Designer: Linda Dingler

Library of Congress Catalog Card Number 82-74174
ISBN 0-06-859835-1

83 84 85 86 87 10 9 8 7 6 5 4 3 2 1

To our parents, Jack and Floss, Lil and Rube, who laid the foundation for who we are to-day; and to our children, Joshua and Nicole, who have added such joy and meaning to our lives.

ACKNOWLEDGMENTS

A heartfelt thank you to all the staff at Canter and Associates who helped make this book possible. Special thanks to Barbara Schadlow, and, of course, Carol Provisor, my editor. We appreciate the feedback from Janie Ornstein, Ph.D., and Nancy and Richard Levine, and, in addition, the support of Harold Roth, our agent, and Eugene Clarke at Harper & Row. Finally, we acknowledge the educators and parents throughout the nation without whose interest and support this book would not exist. Thank you all!

CONTENTS

APPENDIXES

INTRODUCTION

Assertive Discipline is the outgrowth of our combined twenty years of professional experience in helping parents and teachers to deal more effectively with the behavior of children. We brought to these efforts expertise as a teacher (Marlene Canter) and as a family–child counselor (Lee Canter).

Our initial thrust with Assertive Discipline was in the area of education. We wrote several books, including *Assertive Discipline: A Take Charge Approach for Today's Educator* and the *Assertive Discipline Resource Guide.* We developed a training workshop designed to help teachers and administrators eliminate the number one problem they face—discipline. We can gladly state that our Assertive Discipline Program has been an unqualified success. As of 1982, we and our staff have trained close to 300,000 educators (over 10 percent of all educators) from every state in the nation. The Assertive Discipline program has been endorsed or cosponsored by teacher and administrator associations in twenty-five states. Our program had received recognition from the national press, *Newsweek, U.S. News and World Report, Instructor Magazine, National Elementary Principal,* and numerous local newspapers and TV and radio stations. Most important, almost daily we receive calls and letters from grateful educators thanking us for assisting them in their efforts to help the children they teach and guide.

As the success of Assertive Discipline for educators grew, we received an ever-increasing number of requests to offer a program for parents. It was logical for us to develop this program since our early efforts had focused on helping parents as well as educators. Our Assertive Discipline for Parents workshops and this book are the results of our efforts. Assertive Discipline for Parents workshops have already enabled thousands of parents to take charge at home, to the benefit of both themselves and their children. This book is the natural outgrowth of these highly successful workshops.

We want to make a few points before we get into our discussion of Assertive Discipline for Parents. For the purpose of clarity we have addressed the majority of this book towards two-parent families. Throughout the book, though, you will find examples and questions related to the unique challenges encountered by single parents. Finally, we want to state clearly that the techniques and concepts presented in this book are designed to be utilized successfully by all parents.

Next, many parents equate the term *discipline* with hitting or spanking their children. We do not. We define *discipline* as a corrective action designed to help teach children more appropriate behavior. Under no circumstances should the discipline violate the physical or emotional well-being of the children.

Finally, we ourselves are parents, and our own experience has proved that the use of the philosophy and techniques presented in this book has been an invaluable aid in raising our children. But we want to add that Assertive Discipline is not a foolproof method that will enable us—or you—to be successful in all our interactions with our children. Parenting, in our opinion, is the greatest challenge an individual can attempt. We are all human, and no human is perfect. Thus, in raising our children we do the best we can despite the imperfections innate in all of us. Though Assertive Discipline is not a panacea for dealing with your children's behavior, it will prove a tremendous aid that can significantly lessen your struggle to be a good parent.

WHAT IS ASSERTIVE DISCIPLINE?

1

TAKE CHARGE
AND BE THE BOSS

I'll be honest with you, there are times I really feel like I can't handle my kids. The way my kids carry on is simply too much for me. I talk and they just don't listen. I'm lost, I'm overwhelmed, and I'm scared.

—Mother of two, ages seven and ten

I've tried everything I can think of to get my children to behave. I talk to them, I listen to them, I help them express their feelings, I reason with them, and they still act up and talk back day-in and day-out. I'm just at my wits' end.

—Father of three, ages four, eight, and eleven

My kids are just too strong-willed for me or their teacher to handle. It seems that every day I get a call from school about how bad one of them has been. The teachers ask me to do something with my kids and all I can honestly say is that I don't know what to do. I can't describe how frustrating this is for me.

—Mother of two, ages twelve and fourteen

Every day we hear comments like these from parents we work with. Why is this so? More and more of today's parents are expressing how overwhelmed and powerless they feel in dealing with the misbehavior of their children. At times it seems that we are encountering a generation of children who are so strong-willed that

15

in many ways they are controlling the parents who are supposed to be leading and guiding them. The result we observe in all too many families is chaos.

At the same time that so many parents are expressing their feelings of frustration and helplessness, there are other parents who demonstrate that they are fully capable of getting their children to behave. You may ask, "Why do these parents get their children to do what they want them to?" We asked the same question ourselves, and after years of careful examination of parent/child interactions, we found what we believe is the answer. Parents who are effective with their children possess the skills and confidence necessary to clearly and firmly communicate their wants and needs to their children. The parents are prepared to stand up to their children's misbehavior in a firm, no-nonsense, and caring manner. These parents basically *assert* their authority with their children.

In Assertive Discipline we have taken the skills we have learned from these effective parents and combined them into a systematic program designed to enable parents to take charge of their children's misbehavior. This program will give you, the parent, the confidence that is necessary to lay down the law in a firm, consistent and caring manner. Assertive Discipline will teach you two key concepts. *First, you, the parent, must assert your parental authority and be the boss when your children misbehave. Second, in order for you to do so, you will need to develop a systematic plan of action for how you will take charge with your children.*

For your sake and the sake of your children you must be able to take charge and be the boss when your children will not do what you want. What do we mean by "take charge" and "be the boss"? From our work with parents we have determined that most of them who are effective respond to their children's misbehavior with a firm, assertive statement, "I want you to stop that immediately!" These parents are also fully prepared to back up their words with action to ensure that their children comply with their demands: "If you do not stop, you will choose to stay in your room!"

When you take charge by responding in a forceful manner to

your children's misbehavior, you send them this clear message: "I care too much about you to tolerate your misbehavior. I also care too much about myself to allow you to disregard what I tell you to do. I will therefore do everything appropriate and necessary to ensure that you do behave!"

REASONS FOR ASSERTIVE DISCIPLINE

Why must you take charge and be the boss when your children's misbehavior demands it? From our work with families we have found the following reasons. First, for their emotional well-being all children need firm, consistent limits. Your children need to know what they may and may not do. They need to know that you are concerned enough about them to put in the time and effort to make sure that they behave in an acceptable, responsible manner.

We have all seen the results with children who come from homes where the parents are unable or unwilling to set necessary limits. These children are often labeled "brats," "little terrors," or "incorrigible." It is very common for children who do not have the limits that they need to act up in an attempt to get their parents to take notice and lay down the law. This point is poignantly illustrated by the comments of a perceptive thirteen-year-old girl we recently worked with:

> "At first I really thought it was neat the way my parents let me do what I wanted. But then when I got older I began to wonder why they allowed me to do things none of my friends' parents did. You know, I began to really feel they just didn't care about what I did. I even got into trouble to see what they would do, and I couldn't believe they didn't do anything but give me one of their dumb talks. I really wish my parents would stop acting like my friends and start acting like parents."

The second reason you must be the boss is that unless you are able to take charge to get your children to behave, you will soon become frustrated and angry with your children. It is hard to find a parent who does not eventually become resentful of children who overtly or covertly challenge the parent's authority by continually misbehaving.

Your resentment can prove to be a barrier between you and your children. How can you be close to your children if your interactions are frequently punctuated with bitter words, arguments, or threats? How can you express your love and caring to your children if you are constantly angry at them for their misbehavior? How can you serve as a positive role model for your children if your frustrations drive you to lash out at them verbally or physically?

In addition, your children need you to stand up for what you want. They need you to teach them that a parent is someone who must be listened to and respected and that the consequences of disobeying your wishes will be unpleasant. They need you to be in the position to guide them and teach them right from wrong. They need you to teach them that you are prepared to stand up to their anger, their pleas, and their tears, because you have the right and responsibility to do what you feel is best for them. They need you to teach them that you care too much about them to allow them to misbehave without demanding that they stop!

Being the boss also means your taking charge and actively providing your children positive feedback and support when they do behave. Positive feedback is vital if your children are to develop a positive self-image. They need you to teach them that they will receive constant reinforcement when they do behave. They need you to teach them through your words and actions that you are prepared to "catch them being good." Your consistent, positive, and limit-setting feedback will provide them the boundaries of the behaviors you will or will not accept and tolerate. These boundaries help to give your children the structure which all children want and need and which is the foundation for their psychological and emotional growth.

If you have found it difficult at times, or frequently, to be the boss when your children's behavior demands it, don't fret—you are not alone. Many, if not most, of today's parents are in the same position. You may ask why this is so. There are several roadblocks to assertive parent behavior. First, you may feel uncomfortable responding in a forceful, assertive manner, because you have been led to believe it is not in the best interests of your children to do so. Second, you may think that your children have such terrible problems that they can't behave, so there is no point in even trying to get them to do so. Finally, you may simply not know how to respond forcefully. We will examine each of these roadblocks in detail in the next chapter.

If you have had or are at present experiencing difficulty responding forcefully to your children, you may ask, "How can I take charge with my children?" "How do I become the boss with my children?" Thus we come to the goal of Assertive Discipline—to help you to take charge at home by becoming more assertive.

How will being assertive help you, the parent, take charge with your children? When you are assertive, as we have stated, you clearly and firmly communicate your wants and needs to your children: "I want you to follow my directions right now!" Simply stated, you say what you mean and mean what you say. We have found that this kind of direct response will maximize your ability to get your children to stop their misbehavior and behave as you desire.

Being assertive also means being prepared to back up your words with action. With most children who have disregarded what you want and continuously misbehave, your actions will speak louder than words. You will need to let your children know that you are concerned enough about their misbehavior to have consequences ready to use if they choose not to comply with your requests. "If you do not follow my directions, you cannot watch TV until you are ready to do as I have asked."

Finally, being assertive means you are prepared to let your children know how much you appreciate it when they do comply with what you request. "I really like the way you are doing what I ask today."

ASSERTIVE DISCIPLINE PLAN

The key to becoming more assertive is to develop an Assertive Discipline Plan. An Assertive Discipline Plan is a systematic blueprint designed to guide you in dealing with your children's misbehavior. This plan will enable you to determine what behaviors you want your children to change, how you will assertively communicate your wants to your children, and what the consequences will be if they do, or do not, comply.

When your everyday approaches to dealing with your children have failed to produce results, you will need to develop and utilize an Assertive Discipline Plan. To help explain what we mean, we will follow the efforts of a set of parents who recently attended one of our workshops.

Ted and Margie were completely frustrated at their inability to deal with their ten-year-old son, Daniel. He was a strong-willed boy who stubbornly refused to get along with his parents or sister. Ted and Margie had tried everything from talking, reasoning, begging, and pleading, to yelling and screaming, and even, on occasion, taking away all of Daniel's privileges. All these efforts had been in vain. At our workshop, the father threw up his hands and stated, "Daniel just does not care what we do. I don't know what's wrong with the boy. Even when we threaten to punish him, he just sits there and says, 'So?' We just don't know what more we can do."

What Daniel's parents needed to do was to put the time and effort in to develop a plan of action which would let their son know that his behavior must stop. After attending our workshop, they did just that.

When Ted and Margie had determined their plan of action to deal with Daniel they sat down with him and told him in a firm, no-nonsense manner, "Daniel, we are not comfortable with the way you talk to us and to your sister. We expect you to stop your arguing and fighting. We are serious about this, so serious that we promise that we will send you to your room every time you choose to argue and fight with anyone in this family."

From that moment on, each of Daniel's angry outbursts was greeted with a firm "You must stop your arguing. Go to your room!"

When Daniel did cooperate, his parents quickly responded with sincere appreciation. "Daniel, we really like how cooperative you have been today." The parents' concern for their son, which they demonstrated by consistently providing him with limits and praise, resulted in a dramatic improvement in his behavior, to the benefit and relief of all concerned.

Through Assertive Discipline we are going to show that you, too, can influence your children to behave. You no longer have to live with the anguish, frustration, and despair that parents feel when they believe they have little or no control over their children's disruptive, defiant, or destructive behavior. You no longer have to beg and plead pathetically with your children to shape up. You no longer have to assault your children—verbally or physically—in a vain attempt at parental control. You are not helpless. You are not powerless. You are not alone.

Through Assertive Discipline, you will learn to recognize how effective a parent you already are. For example: Why is it that you have been so effective in getting your children to bathe regularly, yet never seem able to stop their fighting? Why is it that you have been so effective in getting your children to behave properly at the table but can never seem to get them to clean their rooms? Why is it that you have been so effective in getting your children to behave so well at other people's houses, but never seem to stop their acting so awful at home?

Through Assertive Discipline you will learn to "take charge" at home in a firm, yet positive manner. Assertive Discipline does not advocate your storming around the house and "throttling" your children whenever they open their mouths. What Assertive Discipline does advocate is that you set firm, consistent limits while, at the same time, recognizing your children's needs for love, affection, and positive support.

Assertive Discipline is not a "cure-all" for every problem that may arise with your children. We don't think that a cure-all exists. Assertive Discipline was designed for all parents who want to develop better skills in dealing with their children's behavior. The goal of Assertive Discipline is to help parents take charge *before* the problems with their children get out of hand. This book was not written for parents of teenagers who have severe behavioral or emotional problems. Assertive Discipline can help those parents, but it should not be used as a substitute for professional counseling or specialized parent-support groups.

Finally, changing how you respond to your children is not easy, and please don't take anything we write to even hint that it is so. We are well aware, from our own experiences, that, for many reasons, we get into habits of responding in one way or another to our children. One does not simply read a book, "see the light," and change like magic. Being aware of how hard it is to change habits, we have structured this book to provide you with as much support and guidance as we can.

SOME QUESTIONS PARENTS ASK RELATED TO TOPICS IN THIS CHAPTER

Question: I feel that by demanding my children just "stop" their problem behavior, I will never deal with the feelings that lie behind their actions. How do you respond to this?

Response: It is vital, even critical, for parents to deal with their children's feelings. We are not suggesting you don't! When they misbehave, your children are challenging your authority, disrupting the household, and acting in a self defeating manner. You must be able to be firm and get them to stop this inappropriate behavior. Once things are under control, it is your responsibility as a loving parent to sit down with your children and help them explore, express, and deal with the feelings that lie behind, and that may cause, their problem behavior.

Question: When I tell my children to do something, they always say they will. They never argue or hassle me. The problem is they do not do what they say they will. What can I do about this?

Response: There is no way you are going to get your children to do what you want unless you follow up on your request. Your children obviously have learned that when you tell them to do something, you do not back up your words with actions to ensure that they comply. If you want to take charge, you are going to have to devise a plan of action to make certain your children do what they say they will.

Question My daughter is constantly in trouble at home and at school. Whenever I do assert myself as you say and discipline her in a firm, consistent manner, she does improve her behavior. The problem is that she gets very upset with me and accuses me of being unfair and overly harsh. After a few days of listening to her I tend to back down, and the problems begin all over again. What do you suggest?

Response: Your daughter obviously has found a way to manipulate you when you lay down the law. Don't feel bad—you are not alone. Many parents react as you do. The message we want to send you is that, even though your daughter may be unhappy with you, you are doing the right thing. There is nothing you can do that is more harmful to your child than to allow her to continue to misbehave without responding in a firm, consistent manner. Keep up the firm, consistent limits. Be sure to balance them with praise when your daughter improves her behavior. If you stick to your guns, we'll wager that after a few days your daughter will stop her complaining.

Question: When I demand that my son do what I want he just smirks and walks away. What do you have to say about this situation?

Response: Our question to you is: What do you do when your son walks away? You are not going to be the boss with a child like this if you tolerate his walking away from you when you lay down the law. We worked with a mother who had a problem similar to yours, and later she reported the following incident. On one occasion when her son walked away from her she grabbed him firmly by the arm, looked him in the eye, and told him, "You will never do that again!" We asked her what she would have done if her son hadn't listened to her, and she told us, "I was prepared to pull out all the stops. I would have grounded him for as long as it took for that boy to realize he could never, ever talk to me that way again." Such sincere determination may be necessary for you to get your point across to your child. Later in the book we will be helping you to come up with a plan of action to deal with this kind of problem.

Question: I'm divorced and whenever I discipline my children they get upset and demand to go live with their father. What do you suggest?

Response: This is not an uncommon problem. You are going to have to let your children know that when they are with you they will have to behave in a manner that you feel is in their best interests. Many children use threats of wanting to go to the other parent as a means to manipulate the disciplining parent into giving in. If this is the case with you, for your best interests, and their best interests we recommend you stand your ground.

2

ROADBLOCKS TO TAKING CHARGE AND BEING THE BOSS

What stops you from taking charge and being the boss when your children's misbehavior demands it? As we have stated, there are several roadblocks that hinder many parents. First, you may feel uncomfortable coming on in a strong, direct manner when your children misbehave. Second, you may think that your children have problems which prevent them from behaving, so you believe there is no point in even trying to assert yourself. And finally, you do not possess the skills to enable you to respond in a forceful manner. Let's examine each of these roadblocks in more detail.

RELUCTANCE TO COME ON STRONG

When a parent responds in a take-charge manner, as we have said, he or she typically responds to the child with a firm, direct statement: "I want you to do it now!" We are well aware that many parents feel they are failures if they have to respond so forcefully in order to get their children to do what they want. We recently observed in a park a child who would not clean up his belongings. His mother told him numerous times to "please clean up," to no avail. Finally, she walked up to him and firmly asserted: "Enough of this. Clean up your things this minute!" The child quickly complied with her demand. The mother, however looked at her friend, shook her head, and said, "Gosh, I hate to have to come on so strong with him. Maybe I'm doing something wrong?"

Many, if not most, parents feel as this mother did because they have been told by contemporary child-rearing experts that for the well-being of their children, no matter how badly they behave, the parents should avoid "stern" or "authoritarian" actions and find alternative approaches. These alternative psychological approaches include talking to their children about why they misbehave (counseling approach), negotiating with their children to change the problem behavior (democratic approach), praising their children when they behave (behavior modification approach), and allowing their children to suffer the natural consequences of their behavior (logical consequences approach). *Each of these approaches has merit; yet all have drawbacks.* Let's discuss these approaches in more detail.

Counseling advocates that parents try to handle their children's problem behavior much as a professional counselor would. The parents should help their children deal with the emotional conflicts and express the negative feelings that cause them to act in an inappropriate manner. We worked with a very bright, sophisticated mother who typifies this approach. She was at her wits' end trying to deal with her ten-year-old son's frequent angry outbursts. She told us she felt her son's behavior was due to his life-long inability to cope with stress in an appropriate manner. During one of our meetings with the two of them, the boy got upset and began to yell at his mother, "I don't have to do what you say. You don't know what you're talking about." His mother responded, "You sure are angry. I'll bet what I said upset you." Her son angrily retorted, "Who cares what you say!"

It may be appropriate for a counselor to respond to children in such an empathetic manner, but we question its value for some parents. It is vital to try to explore the causes of your children's misbehavior, but the limitations of this approach are clear. There are going to be times when, try as you might, you will not be able to determine why your child is misbehaving. Or you may determine what you think is the cause of the child's problems, and it may turn out to be something you can do nothing about—a past trauma, the parents' divorce, etc. Consequently, you might do your best to help the child deal with feelings about the problems, yet he or she will continue to misbehave. Thus you will reach the point where you are stuck. Your children continue to misbehave—and what do you do?

The *democratic approach* dictates that parents deal with their children as "equals" and come up with a mutually agreeable solution to their children's misbehavior. For example, your children want to run through the family room and yell while you and your company want to talk. The way to handle this misbehavior is to sit down with your children and say something like this, "I know you want to run and yell, but I'm not comfortable with the noise. What do you think we can do to solve this problem?" A typical solution would be for the children to decide to make their noise outside.

This approach assumes that all children are reasonable and cooperative, and this is an excellent approach for dealing with children who possess these qualities. This approach breaks down however, when you try to use it with children who are acting unreasonably or uncooperatively, as most children will from time to time. For example, what do you do if your children agree to make noise outside, but quickly change their minds and again disrupt your conversation? You will once again reach the point where you need a response to misbehavior.

Behavior modification is another popular approach to handling children's misbehavior. This is a highly controversial approach that has been widely misinterpreted. Most parents interpret this approach as advocating that parents should reward their children when they behave and that, basically, they should ignore their children when they misbehave. Most parents understand this approach to mean that if you are positive about how you respond to your children, you can get them to behave. For example, we knew parents who had a problem with their daughter's refusing to get to school on time. They set up a plan which awarded her a point whenever she was ready for school on time. When she had earned five points, she could go shopping for a blouse as a reward.

This approach can prove highly useful in helping most children to improve their behavior. However, the approach does have its limitations. What would the parents in the example do if their child still refused to get ready for school on time? What do you do if your child says to you, "I don't care if you reward me, I still will not do what you want." Again, we ask you, what would you do?

The use of the *logical consequences* approach advocates that parents allow their children to suffer the natural consequences that result from misbehavior. It is thought that these consequences will prove so unpleasant for the children that they will eventually choose to behave appropriately. For example, if your child would not do his schoolwork and homework, let him suffer the logical consequence, which would be to fail.

This approach, as with others, can and will work with most children. The problem, as with other approaches, is as follows: What do you do if your child does not care about the logical consequences? What do the parents in the example do if their child could not care less if he fails? There are times when you may face your children still not behaving, no matter what the logical consequences are.

Counseling, democratic approaches, behavior modification, and logical consequences approaches, as we have stated, are all at times useful approaches with most children. None of these approaches, however, provides you with an answer to the problem of what to do when your child still will not behave. What we are saying in Assertive Discipline is that, for those times when all else fails, it is appropriate and necessary that you put aside all your other approaches and recognize that your children need you to assertively demand that they stop their disruptive and destructive behavior.

BELIEF THAT CHILD CAN'T BEHAVE

Another reason you may not take charge with your children is that you misguidedly feel they have emotional, psychological, or physical problems that make it impossible for them to behave.

We recently worked with a couple, Helen and Larry, who were concerned about the "psychological problems" of their children. They told us as follows: "Our children are just upset all the time. They can't control their tempers. If they don't get their way, they get so frustrated they just explode. They yell, scream, and at times even throw things. It's awful, dealing with them when they get upset. We feel we have to walk on eggshells when we're around our children." The parents went on to add, "The children just can't help it. They've always had emotional problems. We honestly feel we never gave them the love and security they needed to develop like other children. There really isn't much we can do until our children work their problems out."

These parents really believe that their children have such terrible "problems" that their angry outbursts are beyond the children's control; in other words, the children can't control their own behavior. If any parent honestly feels this way, it would logically follow that the parent would not be able to get the children to behave. It would make no sense to take charge and demand the children control their tempers if the parent feels there is no way the children can do so.

If you believe that your children can't behave, you will without realizing it give up your parental authority and therefore be in a volatile and frustrating position. This frustration may result in your verbally lashing out at your children. Or you may try to "beat the problem out of them."

On the other hand, your frustration may take the form of "sticking your head in the sand" and denying or ignoring the problem. You may pretend your children are tired, when it's too painful to admit they are obviously "stoned" or drunk. You may choose not to respond to notes from your children's teachers referring to their problem behavior. You may refuse to discuss with your spouse his or her complaints regarding the behavior of your children. You may try to blame the neighbors for not being more tolerant of your children's inappropriate behavior.

If you have experienced these kinds of frustrations in dealing with your children, you are not alone. All too many parents feel their children have problems which prevent them from behaving. For example:

The child is going through a *difficult phase or stage*. You will hear parents state, "He is just intolerable since he turned two." Or, "The kid has been just awful since she started the seventh grade."

The child has a *genetic problem*. In other words the child was born with a problem related to his or her inherited genetic makeup. For example, you will hear parents state, "My daughter has been impossible to handle since birth. She was just born acting that way." Or, "He is a real chip-off-the-old-block. His dad acted the same way when he was young. What can you expect coming from that family?"

The child has suffered an *emotional trauma*. You will hear parents say things such as, "He has just been impossible ever since the divorce. It has made him uncontrollable." Or, "She just never got over the death of her mom. That's why she acts the way she does."

The children are influenced by their *peers*. Parents will say, "When she is with her friends she will do whatever they say—right or wrong." Or, "Ever since he started hanging out with that group of kids, there's nothing I can do with him."

Moms and Dads, it does not matter what problems your children have, or you believe they have. They *can* control their behavior—they *do not want to*. In reality, the only children who cannot control aspects of their behavior are those with organic problems.

A child with epilepsy cannot control the seizures, and to demand that he or she do so would be senseless.

A child with cerebral palsy may have such poor motor coordination, that he or she cannot help making a mess at the table. It would be cruel to reprimand the child for such behavior.

We hope that you are aware that there is much more than semantics involved in the "can't" behave versus the "won't" behave issue that we have just raised. As we just stated, if you honestly feel that your children "can't" behave, how in the world can you ever get them to do so? If, on the other hand, you are able to recognize that your children "won't" behave, then it is up to you to ASSERT YOUR PARENTAL AUTHORITY IN A MANNER WHICH WILL GET THEM TO BEHAVE!

Let's return to the example of Helen and Larry to illustrate what we mean.

These parents felt their children could not control their tempers due to their emotional problems. In the course of our discussions with the parents, the following dialogue regarding the parents inability to get their children to behave took place between the parents and one of the authors.

Author: Can you think of any time your children can control their tempers?

Larry: No, not really.

Helen (after thinking awhile): Yes I can. The kids really do behave themselves when they are with my parents.

Author: Do you have any idea why?

Helen: You have to understand my parents. They are quite strict. They will not tolerate my kids—or any kids—yelling and screaming in their house.

Author: How do they stop your children from having tantrums if they don't get their way?

Larry: Her parents do not play around. They are very matter-of-fact with the kids. If the children started to have tantrums my in-laws would probably just tell them firmly to "Please be quiet!"

Author: What do you think Grandma and Grandpa would do if your children continued to have tantrums?

Helen: Well, when the kids were younger and did not listen to their grandparents and got really wild, my folks immediately sent them home. You know, come to think about it, they have not had any problems with my kids since.

Author: Does either of you ever come on as assertively with your children as Grandma and Grandpa do?

Helen: Not really. It probably just won't do any good. They just get too upset when they're with us.

Larry: Wait a second. I think I hear what you are getting at. Grandma and Grandpa won't put up with their tantrums and really let the kids know this—and, doggone it, the kids don't have tantrums there. Are you saying we need to come on just as strong?

Author: Well what do you think? You are the parents.

Helen: You know, I think you are right. If the kids can behave with my folks, there really is no reason why they cannot behave with us. I think we've been so worried about their emotional problems that we have not done what needs to be done. The kids can control their tempers, but they don't want to. We have to come on like my folks do and make them!

Following our meeting with the parents, they went home and proceeded to demand assertively that their children stop their tantrums and then consistently responded by sending their children to their rooms each time they did not control their tempers. Within a few weeks, their children's behavior was dramatically improved.

NOT KNOWING HOW TO TAKE CHARGE

The final reason that prevents some parents from not firmly taking charge with their children is that they just do not know how to do so. If you are like most parents, you have probably had no training in how to be a parent. You have probably had no training in recognizing what will, or will not, work when it comes to disciplining children. You may be trying to deal with children who behave towards you very differently from the way you behaved towards your parents. We continually hear parents say, "My children act in a manner I would never have thought of doing." One father told us, "My children say and do things I would never even think of."

The net result of this change is that you may be at a loss for how to handle your children's misbehavior. Your learned approaches to discipline may not work, and all the new approaches you have read or heard about also may prove ineffective. In other words, you lack the needed skills and confidence to take charge firmly. Through Assertive Discipline we will present to you the specific skills you need to let your children know what it is you want them to do —and how to make sure they do it!

• In this chapter we have discussed the roadblocks to your taking charge and being the boss with your children. Here is the main point we want you to remember: *A child's upbringing, genetic make-up, stage of development, and peer pressure definitely influence his or her behavior but do not control it.* We will demonstrate in the following chapters how, through the use of Assertive Discipline, you can still take charge with these children and get them to behave.

SOME QUESTIONS PARENTS ASK RELATED TO TOPICS IN THIS CHAPTER

Question: My children say I am mean and they become upset when I respond to them in what you describe as an assertive manner. If what I am doing is right, why do they get so upset?

Response: Your children are testing your limits. Children always want to know if you truly mean business. In the past they may have learned that if they raise a big fuss and cause you enough hassles, you will back down. It is in your best interest, as well as your children's, to resist their attempts to manipulate you. Stand up for your wants and needs and do what you feel is best.

Question: My son simply falls apart when I discipline him the way you outline. It hurts me to see this. Isn't there an easier way to handle these problems?

Response: Let's be honest. There is nothing more difficult than disciplining your children. It hurts! Do you remember your parents telling you in the old saying, "It hurts me more than it hurts you," after they disciplined you? As a parent, you realize there is great truth in that saying. The issue is, do you care enough about your children to endure the unpleasant feelings and do what is needed to provide them with appropriate limits for their inappropriate behavior.

Question: Don't you feel you must understand why your children are misbehaving before you can realistically help them change their behavior?

Response: Ideally, you would want to know why your children are misbehaving before you attempted to help them change their behavior. There is one major problem in this concept. With most children we can do no more than speculate as to why they are misbehaving. One school of thought maintains that the cause of children's misbehavior may be a result of their early feeding habits, toilet training, or relations with their mother and father. Even if you knew one of these past experiences was the cause, what good would it do you? Rather than putting extensive energy into determining why your children are misbehaving, place that same energy into formulating a plan of action for how you will deal with it. You will benefit from this approach and so will your children.

Question: My wife and I have been divorced for three years and, to say the least, she does not believe in disciplining the children. When they come to spend the weekend with me, they act like wild animals. I don't like being the bad guy and laying down the law. Do you have any other suggestions?

Response: Please do not feel you are the "bad guy" when you expect your children to act appropriately. In the long run your children will come to appreciate the fact that you care enough about them to expect them to behave in an appropriate manner when they are with you on the weekend.

Questions: I feel my child's problems are directly related to the fact that I am a working mother. What do you have to say about this?

Response: We are very tired of hearing that because a mother works, the children will have problems. There is no direct relationship between the two conditions. Just because you work does not mean you are incapable of dealing with your child's behavior.

3

ASSERTIVE–NONASSERTIVE– HOSTILE RESPONSES

In explaining Assertive Discipline, we want to start with a description of effective and ineffective responses parents make both when their children misbehave and when they behave. We label the effective responses of parents *assertive* and the ineffective responses *nonassertive* and *hostile*.

HOW DO YOU RESPOND WHEN YOUR CHILDREN MISBEHAVE?

Let's begin our explanation by focusing on how parents can assertively respond to their children's misbehavior.

Assertive Responses

How should you respond to your children when their behavior is such a problem to you, themselves, or others that you feel the problem must stop? Through our years of professional and clinical experience we have determined that when parents are determined that their children behave, they address their children with a direct, *assertive* statement.

> I want no more playing around. You will go to bed right now!

> I cannot accept your being late to school. You will go to school on time every day.

> No more excuses. You will get your chores done right now.

An assertive statement sends the children this message: You are expected to do what I want you to. Implicit in the statement is that you are prepared to follow through with actions to ensure your children's compliance.

> If your child does not comply with your statement to go to bed, you may take him by the hand and put him in his bed.

> If your child does not comply with your statement to stop being late to school, you may drive her to school and make sure she goes to class on time.

> If your child does not comply with your statement to do his chores, you may forbid him to play or watch TV until the chores are finished.

For clarity's sake we label a firm, clear statement—one that you are prepared to back up with actions—an *assertive response*. An assertive response enables you to take charge with your children. This kind of response will maximize your ability to get your children to behave but will not violate the children's best interests.

It is vital that you understand how your assertive responses will enable you to increase your ability to respond effectively when you want your children to shape up. On the other hand, in order to improve how you handle your children, it is equally important that you are aware of why other responses you attempt may prove ineffective. We label ineffective responses as either *nonassertive* or *hostile*.

Nonassertive Responses

Nonassertive responses are ineffective because the parents do not clearly state what they want to their children or, if they do, they are not prepared to back up their words with action. When parents respond in a nonassertive manner, they allow their children to take advantage of them because they communicate to the children that they do not mean business and are not prepared to take firm action.

We want to help you understand why nonassertive responses tend to be ineffective. In order to do so, here are examples of typical nonassertive responses parents may make to their children's misbehavior and why the responses do not work.

Statement of Fact: "You're Still Not Doing What I Want."
Many parents feel that it is useful to point out to their children that they are misbehaving.

> You're talking back again.
> Your chores have not been done.
> You got into trouble again at school today.

This response assumes your children are not aware of what they are doing and that if they were, they would stop their misbehavior. Unfortunately, most children are fully aware that they are doing something you do not want them to do, and telling them what they are doing does not communicate what you really want, which is for them to stop.

Questioning: "Why Are You Doing That?"
Most of today's parents feel that if they can determine the cause of their children's misbehavior, they can stop it. In theory this principle is sound; in practice it rarely works. Most young children do not know why they are misbehaving and most older children give you reasons you probably will not like.

Parent to Young Child: Why don't you behave at school?

Child: I don't know.

Parent to Young Child: What's bothering you?

Child: Nothing.

Parent to Older Child: Why don't you listen to me?

Child: I don't want to!

Parent to Older Child: Why are you yelling and screaming at everyone again?

Child: I feel like it because I hate all of you!

Parents may also respond to their children's misbehavior with other types of ineffective questions.

How many times do I have to tell you to stop talking back?
What am I going to do with you?
Are you ever going to stop carrying on?

No matter what types of questions you utilize in response to your children's misbehavior, they do not communicate your true desire—that your children behave.

Unclear Goals: "Try to Behave."
It is not uncommon for parents to respond to their children's misbehavior with vague, indirect goals such as:

I don't ever want to catch you fighting with your sister again.

I want you to think about how bad you acted at school.

You must try to behave better.

All of these goals are well-intentioned, but they are usually ineffective. "I don't ever want to catch you fighting with your sister again" does not tell the child to stop fighting but to fight at some time you will not catch him. "I want you to think about how bad you acted at school" does not communicate to the child to stop misbehaving at school but just to think about the behavior. And finally, "You must try to behave better" does not tell the child to stop, but just to try.

You may object at this point and assert that your children really do know you want them to stop their misbehavior even when you make an indirect response such as a statement of fact, a question, or asking them to try. We have, however, found that while your children understand the thrust of your message—that you want them to stop their misbehavior—they are experts at tuning in on whether or not you mean business. Your children can read you like a book. Through years of experience your children have learned that when you question, or make vague remarks, like most parents you are not intent on "laying down the law." You probably will not back up these responses with the firm disciplinary actions you would use had you made an assertive demand that they behave. Your children pick up that they can probably get away with their misbehavior and continue to challenge your authority.

Demand the Children Behave, But Do Not Follow Through: "How Many Times Do I Have to Tell You!"

Not following through is a classic, nonassertive response to misbehavior. The parent responds with an assertive demand, yet does nothing to make the child comply if the child does not want to.

Susan is watching television again instead of doing her required chores. Her father walks into the room and observes her.

Father: Susan, stop watching television and get your chores done right now! I'm tired of having to talk to you about this.

Susan: O.K., Dad, I'll do them.

A few minutes later her father returns and she is still watching television.

Father: Susan, I told you to do your chores. Now turn off that TV and do them.

Susan: You're right, Dad. I'll do them.

Father again returns in a few minutes and she is still watching television.

Father: Doggone it, Susan. I told you to turn off that TV and do your chores! I've had it with you. You never listen to me!

Ignore the Problem: "There's Nothing I Can Do, So Why Try?"
Some parents feel so inadequate attempting to deal with their children's misbehavior that they ignore it as though it had never occurred.

We observed a woman in a market with her two children who were repeatedly using "four-letter" words in their conversation. After some time the woman's friend turned to her in a perturbed manner and asked, "Don't you hear the words your kids are using?" The mother replied, "I don't pay any attention anymore. I've tried to stop them, but they just won't listen to me, so why bother?"

As you can see nonassertive responses can range from indirect statements and firm demands that are not followed through on to just ignoring the behavior. What they all have in common is the lack of impact needed to communicate to your children you do mean business.

Hostile Responses

The second type of ineffective response is hostility. Hostile responses are those parents make which are designed to get their children to behave, while disregarding the children's needs and feelings. When parents respond in this way their manner communicates to the children "I don't like you." Often when parents respond in a hostile manner, they are trying to "get back" at their children rather than to help them behave. Here are examples of typical hostile responses parents utilize.

Verbal Put-downs: "You Make Me Sick."
The parents respond to the misbehavior of their children with angry verbal assaults.

> I can't believe you did something as dumb as that.
> Why don't you ever act good like your sister? You're always bad.
> You always do the wrong thing.
> You should be ashamed of how you act. You're just awful.

Please note, even though the hostile put-downs are very strong statements of your frustration, they do not ever convey what you really want your children to do.

Threats: "You're Going to Get It!"
Many parents when they are frustrated, threaten their children with punishment "if" they continue misbehaving.

> If you act up at school one more time, you've had it!

If you carry on at the market again, I'm going to whip you.

Threats may sound strong, but we have found that most children learn at an early age that phrases such as "if you do that again, I'm going to . . ." are not usually enforced by the parents. The children learn to disregard such messages and continue their misbehavior.

Severe Punishment: "You Can't Leave Your Room for a Week."
When the children misbehave they are punished, often severely. The punishment may be anything the parents feel the children do not want to happen. Often the punishment is designed more for the parents to release their frustration than as a corrective action for the children.

Two parents, Jane and Ralph, reported this to us: Their thirteen-year-old son would periodically leave the house and not tell them he was going away. One day he was gone for a particularly long time and when he returned they exploded. Angrily, they grounded him in the house for "one whole month." Jane told us that by the end of a few days, "I couldn't handle having him around for one more minute. His being stuck in the house was worse for me than it was for him." The parents felt they had to back down from their overly severe punishment and let him go outside.

Physical Response: "I'm Going to Give You What You Deserve."
We have worked with parents who have used such responses as pulling the children's hair, squeezing their arms, throwing them against the wall, or beating them. These are all responses designed to meet the parent's need to release their anger and hurt rather than help set limits for the children.

Just as children learn that their parents do not mean business when they utilize indirect, nonassertive responses, the children learn the same thing regarding the parents' hostile responses. They know that your loud threats and inappropriate punishment are an indication that you probably feel that you cannot get them to behave or are not willing to put in the effort necessary to make them toe the line. Thus your children continue to challenge and battle with you.

HOW DO YOU RESPOND WHEN YOUR CHILDREN DO WHAT YOU WANT?

From our professional experience we have determined that parents can also respond in an assertive, nonassertive, or hostile manner when their children comply with their demands.

Assertive Responses

An assertive response to your children's appropriate behavior is one that enables you to take charge and clearly and firmly communicate to them your positive recognition of their improved behavior. Assertive responses usually include a positive statement to your children.

> I really like the way you followed my directions.
> I was really excited and happy to hear that you behaved so well at school today.
> I really appreciate how well you and your brother are getting along today.

Some parents find it helpful to back up their praise with positive consequences to increase the impact of their assertive message.

You were so cooperative today that I'll read you a special story at bedtime.

You did such a great job doing your chores that you can have ice cream for dessert tonight.

You two did such a good job playing together and cleaning up today that you can stay up half-an-hour later tonight.

Assertive responses to your children's positive behavior are *vital,* for they will let your children know that you will recognize and support them when they do what you want rather than just "get on them" when they misbehave.

Nonassertive Responses

When your children finally do what you want, but you ignore and do not reinforce their improved behavior, we label this a nonassertive response. Many parents who respond in a nonassertive manner state, "I should not have to praise my children for doing what I ask." This kind of passive response does not clearly communicate to your children that they are doing what you want and that you desire this behavior to continue.

Hostile Responses

When children comply with their parents' demands and their parents respond with a sarcastic, negative, or degrading comment, we label this a hostile response. Typical hostile responses sound like this:

I can't believe you listened to me! What's wrong with you?

It's about time you acted like a human being.

So you finally decided to keep your big mouth shut for a while.

Not only do hostile responses do nothing to reinforce children's improved behavior, they usually result in the children quickly reverting to their previous misbehavior.

SAMPLE SITUATIONS

In order to give you practice in discriminating between nonassertive, hostile, and assertive response styles, here are examples of typical situations encountered by parents. For each situation we will provide a typical nonassertive, hostile, and assertive response. These illustrations do not exhaust the possible responses to each situation, nor is the assertive response given the *only* way to respond assertively.

Children Misbehave

The parents have continual hassles with their children's arguing and fighting at the dinner table. As if right on schedule, the children begin arguing as soon as dinner is served.

Nonassertive response
The parents complain, "I just don't know what's wrong with you children. When are you going to stop arguing and carrying on at the dinner table? We just can't take it anymore."

Hostile response
The parents scream at the children, "We are sick and tired of your big mouths. Just shut up!"

Assertive response
The parents firmly tell the children, "Stop arguing and fighting at the dinner table. If you do it again, you choose to finish your meal in your room."

A ten-year-old girl rarely finishes her work at school and is failing. The parents have told her that if she has not finished her work at school, she must finish it at home and cannot visit her friends or use the phone until the work is completed. She arrives home with a note from her teacher stating that again her work has not been completed at school.

Nonassertive response

The parent asks, "What's wrong with you? Why didn't you do your work again? Come on, you know how to behave. I'm tired of getting these bad reports." The parent does not require the girl to complete the work.

Hostile response

The parent angrily shouts, "I can't believe you didn't do your work again. I have had it with you. I don't care what you do!"

Assertive response

The parent firmly states, "I want you to sit down and do not get up until your work is completed."

A thirteen-year-old repeatedly argued and talked back to his parents. One afternoon his parents ask him to please stop bouncing his basketball in the house. The child angrily retorts, "Quit bugging me. Get off my case. I'll stop when I want to!"

Nonassertive response

The parent asks, "How in the world can you talk to me that way? Who do you think you are? What am I going to do with you?"

Hostile response

The parent angrily grabs the child and shouts, "Keep your big, filthy mouth shut!"

Assertive response
The parent walks up to the child and firmly states, "You will never talk to me that way again. You are grounded for the remainder of the day!"

Once again, you can see in each example that when parents respond in an assertive manner they clearly and firmly communicate their wants and needs and, are prepared if necessary to back up their words with actions.

Children Behave

The parents have had trouble getting their eight-year-old to do his chores without continually reminding him. One day he does all of his chores on his own before his parents come home.

Nonassertive response
The parent does not recognize the fact that he has done what they had requested.

Hostile response
The parent remarks, "It's about time that I didn't have to hassle you about doing your chores."

Assertive response
The parent says, "Hey, we really like how you did your chores on your own. You did such a great job that we are going to give you a quarter bonus on your allowance."

A six-year-old has had difficulty sharing his toys and playing cooperatively. One day his parents observe him playing appropriately with his friends.

Nonassertive response
The parent thinks, "That's the first time I have seen him

play so well with other children for so long." The parent, however, does not communicate this recognition or positive support to the child.

Hostile response

The parent walks up to the child and comments, "It's about time you started playing nicely with your friends. I can't believe you're finally acting nice."

Assertive response

The parent goes up to the child and tells him, "I really like the way you are playing so cooperatively and sharing your toys."

• We would like you to remember these points regarding assertive, nonassertive, and hostile response styles that we have discussed in this chapter. An assertive statement is one that you are prepared to back up with action and is the most effective response you can utilize when your children misbehave. Nonassertive and hostile responses are usually ineffective responses to your children's repeated misbehavior. When your children do behave, it is vital to respond assertively and reinforce them in the good behavior.

SOME QUESTIONS PARENTS ASK RELATED TO TOPICS IN THIS CHAPTER

Question: I've been what you would label a "nonassertive" parent. Won't it have a detrimental effect on my children if all of a sudden I make a dramatic change?

Response: First off, don't run around your house and start wildly sending your children into their room. You will need to sit down with your children and explain to them that their past misbehavior has been unacceptable and what you are going to be doing about it. Next, please do not worry about your children. I guarantee you, they are much more adaptable than you are. The main impact that your being more assertive will have on your children is that they will improve their behavior, stop their "hassling," and have a better relationship with you. We have never heard of children suffering psychological trauma from their parents' becoming more effective in how they deal with them.

Question: It seems to me that most parents I know threaten their children and then don't follow through. What's so wrong with that?

Response: It is a safe bet that if these parents respond as inconsistently as you state, they will often have great difficulty in getting their children to behave in a manner that is in the best interests of both the parents and the children. We'll also guarantee you these parents are frequently frustrated by these interactions with their children.

Question: My dad was plenty hostile with us kids. If we got out of line, he would call us every name in the book, and if that didn't work, he'd whip the living daylights out of us. He sure got us to behave. What's so wrong with that?

Response: We'll answer your question with a question of our own. How did you feel when your dad would either verbally berate or whip you? We'll bet you did not feel too good. What we are saying is that the goal of discipline is to teach children how to behave in a manner that is in their best interests as well as in the parents'. We firmly believe that no individual—adult or child—has the right to verbally or physically abuse another person.

II

THE ASSERTIVE DISCIPLINE PLAN

4

ASSERTIVE DISCIPLINE PLAN: STEP ONE
Determining What You Want Your Children to Do and Communicating Your Goals

When all that you have tried has failed to get your children to behave, you will need to lay down the law assertively. The key to laying down the law is to have a plan of action for how you will do so. We call such a plan of action an Assertive Discipline Plan. This plan consists, first, of what behaviors you will request that your children change and, second, how you will back up your words with action if your children do, or do not, comply with your demands.

Why is an Assertive Discipline Plan needed? When you reach the point with your children's behavior that you need Assertive Discipline, you may be feeling frustrated, overwhelmed, or at a loss for what to do next. Your children will have given you a clear message: "I do not want to do what you want me to!" You may begin to wonder if there is something wrong with your children, or perhaps even yourself, that has caused you to be so ineffective. In other words you will probably lack the necessary confidence to demonstrate to your children that you mean business and you are the boss.

An Assertive Discipline Plan is a confidence-builder. We say this for the following reason. When you have a systematic plan for responding to your children's misbehavior, you are prepared. You know exactly what you want them to do and how to effectively communicate that they must do it: "I want you to follow my directions!" You know, as well, exactly how you will respond if your children do not comply with your requests: "Go to your room." And you know how you will respond if your children do comply: "I really like how you did what I asked."

The more prepared you are, the easier it will be for you to respond in a consistently assertive manner to your children's misbehavior. In order for you to get your children to stop their chronic misbehavior, you will have to respond more consistently than you normally do. Thus, having an Assertive Discipline Plan will prove a vital asset in your efforts to take charge.

In the remainder of this chapter and in the next three chapters, we will discuss in detail the components of an Assertive Discipline Plan and how to implement one with your children. We will begin with how to determine those behaviors you feel you must request your children change. We will then help you to determine what disciplinary consequences you will utilize if your children do not comply with your demands and what positive consequences you will utilize when your children do behave. Finally, we will discuss how you should present your plan to your children and, after you have done so, how to implement it.

Please note: We are aware you may be anxious to get started using Assertive Discipline with your children, but our program is designed to be used in a systematic manner. Thus, we ask that you do not attempt to utilize any of the techniques we present until you have (1) read the remainder of this book and (2) filled out the worksheets and reviewed the resource ideas in the Appendix.

STEP ONE: DECIDE WHAT YOU WANT YOUR CHILDREN TO DO

The first step of an Assertive Discipline Plan is for you to determine how you want your children to behave. What are your children doing that you want them to stop.

Before we go any further we want to emphasize this point. The behavioral goals you have for your children may differ from those of other parents. There is no absolute right or wrong. You have the right and responsibility to determine the rules your children must follow, as long as the rules are not harmful to your children and you are willing to put in the time and effort to enforce them. No friends, relatives, neighbors, or experts can tell you what is best for you and your children. You are the one who has to live with your children. You are the the one who knows what is best for your children. You are the one who knows when your children's behavior crosses your bottom line and must be dealt with firmly. In order to help you determine the behaviors you want to work on, we will present to you the guidelines we have found necessary to follow:

Determine SPECIFIC Behaviors You Want to Work On.

When we ask parents what they want from their children we typically hear responses such as

> I want my children to be good.
> I want my children to show me and my husband respect.
> I don't want my boys to hassle me all the time.

These responses are unclear and vague. What do you mean when you say "be good"? How do you know when your children are showing you "respect"? What do you mean by "hassle"?

To be more effective you must request SPECIFIC BEHAVIORS from your children. By specific behaviors we mean that you say, "Do your chores," or, "Behave at school," rather than, "Act good"; say "Follow directions," or "Don't talk back," rather than, "Show respect"; say "No fighting or yelling," rather than, "No hassles."

When you determine the specific behaviors you want and need from your children, you will be able not only to keep track of whether or not they are complying with your desires, but you will also be able to communicate those desires more effectively to them. Here is what we mean. Read the following two requests from a parent to a child.

1. I want you to stop carrying on.
2. I want you to follow my directions the first time I give them.

Which request better communicated exactly what the parent wanted and needed his or her child to do? The vast majority of parents will choose the second. The first request, "I want you to stop carrying on," is vague. What does the parent mean by "carrying on"? In the second request, the parent clearly states what he or she desires, "Follow my directions the first time I give them." This statement maximizes the impact of the parent's message.

Make a List of the Behaviors You Want from Your Children.

You and your spouse will need to make a list of all the specific behaviors you want your children to engage in. Here are typical behaviors most parents want:

Do what you're told the first time.

No talking back.

Behave at school.

Tell me where you are going.

Keep your room clean.

Do your chores.

Bathe regularly.

Be home on time.

Eat the food I cook.

Clean up your mess.

Do your homework.

No teasing.

No cigarettes, alcohol, or drugs.

Tell the truth.

No whining.

No fighting.

Go to bed on time.

No running or screaming in the house.

Do not take anything that is not yours.

Eat properly at the table.

Both you and your spouse should write down each and every behavior your children engage in that bothers you. See the worksheet in the Appendix.

Determine Behaviors Your Children MUST Change.

Most parents come up with a list of numerous behaviors their children engage in that bother them. You will need to narrow this list down by asking the following questions: Which behaviors cross your bottom line so that you feel your children *must* change them? For example, you may prefer that your children get dressed as soon as they get up, but it is not imperative that they do so. On the other hand, you cannot tolerate your children's continuous arguing with you, and this behavior *must* change.

It is vital that you give a good deal of careful thought to deciding which behaviors your children must change versus those you would prefer they change. Here is why. It may take sincere determination to motivate your children to change their behavior. It is not easy to consistently make and follow through on demands. You're going to have to put yourself out. Your children may get upset with you. One mother summed it up well when she stated,

"When I began to take charge, my kids didn't like the limits and they let me know it in no uncertain terms. It was harder than I had imagined. I'm really glad I picked only problems that were so important that I couldn't back down no matter how hard my kids yelled, cried, and complained."

Start with One or Two Behaviors

Give careful thought to the behaviors your children must change. Make a list of these specific behaviors. Then pick one or, at most, two behaviors per child that you and your spouse want them to change. Do not deal with more than two behaviors initially. Working on too many problems at first can get confusing and possibly overwhelming.

Please note: You and your spouse must agree on which of your children's behaviors you are willing to put forth the time and effort to work on changing. Teamwork is critical. Without teamwork your children will play the old "divide and conquer" game. Agree beforehand on your behaviorial goals and prevent this problem from developing.

Let's summarize the guidelines we have just discussed. The first step of your Assertive Discipline Plan is for you and your spouse to agree upon one or two specific behaviors your children must change.

FAMILY EXAMPLE

In order to further demonstrate how to develop and implement an Assertive Discipline Plan, we will take the case of a typical set of parents. We will follow these parents' efforts, using the resource tools of this book, through all phases of developing and utilizing their Assertive Discipline Plans. We want to state clearly that these parents' methods, though typical, are not the only way to go about utilizing Assertive Discipline. You must decide what will work for you.

Emily and Steve had two children, eleven-year-old Kevin and eight-year-old Karen. Both Emily and Steve tried to be fair and understanding with their children. They always did their best to find alternatives to disciplining their children. But the older their children got, the harder it was to get them to behave. It seemed to Emily and Steve that their children were beginning to run the house. When the parents told them what to do, Karen would say, "O.K." and then go about doing anything but that which she was asked to do. Kevin, on the other hand, would argue just about anytime he was asked to do something. "Why do I have to do that?" "I don't want to," or, "Later!" were his favorite responses.

The parents were becoming aware of other problems as well. Karen would consistently leave her toys and clothes wherever she dropped them. She rarely cleaned up after herself without a great deal of prodding. Kevin was becoming more reluctant to do his homework. His parents had to continually remind him to get it done, and when he did do his homework, it was in a half-hearted manner.

Emily and Steve would talk with their children to try to find out "why" they did not behave. They began to feel they must have done something wrong as parents to have children who had such problems cooperating and following directions.

Eventually, Emily and Steve reluctantly began to discipline their children. In reality, the discipline tended to threats of "next time you do that, you will be sorry." Occasionally, they would take away TV privileges, send the children to their rooms, or make them go to bed early—all to no avail.

It was not long before they found themselves becoming increasingly frustrated and angry with their children. Steve would angrily lash out: "I'm just sick and tired of you two—your attitude stinks!" Emily seemed to nag the children constantly: "Come on kids, you're driving me up the wall." On several occasions her anger spilled over, and she slapped Kevin when he persisted in arguing with her.

Emily and Steve reached the point where they realized something must be done. They knew it was not beneficial for them or their children to be always hassling. They decided they needed to take charge and develop a plan of action for dealing with their children's misbehavior.

They realized that in the past they had been able to get their children to behave when they had responded in a firm, assertive manner. Steve mentioned how they had stopped Kevin from teasing Karen when she had to wear glasses. Their firm demand to "Stop teasing your sister!" which was followed up by his being sent to his room whenever he disobeyed, had produced quick results. Emily and Steve agreed that such firm, assertive responses might prove useful again.

They began their planning efforts by deciding how they wanted their children's behavior to change. Like most parents, at first they came up with vague goals. They wanted their children to change their "lousy attitudes"—Kevin was always "angry" and Karen "couldn't care less." After giving it some thought, Emily and Steve were able to come up with the specific behaviors they wanted each child to change. Here are the lists they devised:

Karen
1. Follow directions the first time.
2. Clean up after herself.
3. Do her chores before dinner.
4. Eat less sweets.

Kevin
1. Follow directions without arguing.
2. Do homework on his own.
3. Do his chores before dinner.
4. Do not eat snacks before dinner.
5. Take a bath or shower every night.

Both parents felt that it was imperative that their children follow directions and that Karen must clean up after herself and Kevin must do his homework. The other problems they thought could be tolerated for now and dealt with later.

The parents ranked the problems to work on and decided that they should first come up with a plan of action to get each child to follow directions. Once they had determined the behaviors they were going to work on, they had completed the first step of their Assertive Discipline Plan for each child.

PLAN HOW TO COMMUNICATE YOUR BEHAVIORAL GOALS TO YOUR CHILDREN

Once you have determined the specific behaviors you want to work on, you will then want to plan how to communicate these goals to your children. There are four general ways of communicating to your children that you want them to behave.

Hint: Everyone should be getting dressed.

"I" message: I want you to get dressed, please.

Question: Would you please get dressed?

Demand: Get dressed right now!

In most instances, when your children *initially* do not do what you want, it is appropriate to utilize a hint, question, or "I" message to communicate your requests. Such methods are usually effective with most children. When these responses fail to get results, as has probably happened in relation to the problem behaviors you are working on, a demand may be needed. A demand differs from the previous responses in a significant manner. A demand implies that punishment will be the consequence for not obeying: "Get dressed now, or else. . . ." Unfortunately, you know that all too often you will make a demand when there is absolutely no way you intend, or are in any way prepared, to follow through with a consequence for noncompliance. This inability to follow through often results in your responding nonassertively, making demand after demand that you are not ready to enforce, with the result that your children learn to disregard your words. Here is an example:

Parent: Kids, it's time for you to do your homework. Stop playing and get to work now, please. (*Two of the children immediately put their game away and start doing their homework. Mark continues to play.*)

Parent: Mark, I was talking to you, too. Do your homework now!

Mark: I will, I will. (*Continues to play with his game.*)

Parent (loudly): Mark, get to work! (*Mark begins to pick up his game very slowly.*)

Mark: (*Stops playing, but does not get out his homework.*)

Parent (angrily): If I have to talk to you one more time, you have had it.

Mark: (*Goes to his desk, sits there, and does not do his work.*)

Parent (frustrated): Mark, I will not tolerate this any longer, I've had it. Get to work!

Mark: (*Picks up a pencil, stares blankly at the paper, and still does not do his homework.*)

Through exchanges like these, the children of this parent, especially Mark, will quickly learn not to listen to their parent's demands. As a result, the parent probably will resort to hostile screaming, name-calling, or physical means to get his or her request met.

The first and only commandment of Assertive Discipline is this: "Thou shalt not make a demand thou art not preparest to follow through upon!" For the sake of your children and of yourself, do not make a demand unless you are *prepared* to back it up with actions. Before you present your children with a demand, ask yourself this one question: What am I prepared to do if my children do, or do not, comply with my demand? If you have responses ready that are both appropriate and assertive, then you are ready to make your demand. If you don't have responses, plan them, then make your demand. Let's look at the example of Mark's not doing his homework. Here is a way the parent could have dealt with him assertively:

> **Parent:** Mark, I was talking to you, too. Do your homework now!
> **Mark:** I will, I will. *(Continues to play with his game.)*
> **Parent** (firmly): Mark, you have a choice. Do your homework now, or you will not watch television the rest of the night.

To recapitulate, these are the points we want you to remember. First, when your hints, questions, or "I" messages fail to produce results, then it is time for a demand. The less you have to use demands the more effective they will be. Second, do not make demands you can't follow through on.

In relation to making your demands, how you show what you want nonverbally is as important as what you say. You communicate just as much through your tone of voice and nonverbal behavior as you do with your words. Learning nonverbal as well as verbal methods to deliver an effective message is a significant step in developing assertive skills. Note how the parent in the following example delivered his demand:

> A father observed his son roughly pushing and shoving his little brother. He sat down with the boy, looked him in the eye, placed a hand on his shoulder, and, told him, "Tom keep your hands to yourself." As he spoke he gestured to add emphasis to his words.

Eye contact, gesture, and use of the child's name are all useful tools in increasing the effectiveness of your verbal communication with your children. Now we will explain why each of these facets is so important.

Eye contact: When you deliver a message in person without making eye contact, the message will be ineffective. Eye contact is vital to human communication. We say as much with our eyes as with our words. You can increase the effectiveness of any message by looking the other individual, especially your child, in the eye when you speak. Whenever possible, make eye contact with your child when you are telling him or her what you want.

Please note: Some children will not want to look you in the eye. This may be due to a number of reasons, including fear, defiance, or culturally learned behavior. You have to decide if it is, or is not, appropriate to make the child look at you by *gently* turning his or her head so your eyes meet.

Hand gesture: Gestures are utilized to emphasize our words. Hand gestures can often communicate nonverbally to the child, "I mean what I am saying." An important point to remember—there is a major difference between a hand gesture designed to emphasize your words and one used to intimidate your child. We are referring especially to shaking your finger in the child's face as you speak. This does little more than frighten the child.

Use of name: Using your child's name when delivering a message personalizes the message, thus increasing its impact. It is particularly significant to use your child's name when he or she is not in close proximity to you. For example, when the children are out in the yard making a disturbance, rather than calling, "You kids outside, stop making such a mess," announce to whom you are specifically directing your comments, "Mike and Steve, stop making such a mess."

Touch: Touch adds the impact of creating physical as well as verbal limits. Placing your hand on your child when you speak is a clear indicator of the sincerity and forcefulness of your message. For some children, your hand on their shoulder will communicate more than words can say.

• In this chapter we have discussed the first step of your Assertive Discipline Plan, determining what you want your children to do. To summarize, if you want to communicate your behavioral goals to your children and maximize the impact of your statement you will need to remember to look your children in the eye, call them by name, and, if appropriate, touch them and gesture when you are delivering your message.

SOME QUESTIONS PARENTS ASK RELATED TO TOPICS IN THIS CHAPTER

Question: My child's behavior at school is abominable, and I must do something about it. I don't know, though, if his problems at home are that serious or just typical behavior for his age. What do you feel that I should do?

Response: If you don't feel the problems at home are serious enough to do anything about, there is no reason to put any effort into trying to get your child to change. Please be aware, if you are not one hundred percent behind your child's changing his behavior at home, he or she will quickly pick up your ambivalence and not respond.

Question: My kids are so bad that I don't know what problems to begin with. What do you suggest?

Response: Focus on those behaviors that bother you the most or are the most disruptive. A key point to be aware of is that as you begin to deal with your children's most serious problems, you will notice the children beginning to shape up in areas in which you are not even working.

Question: My son is in therapy, and his counselor feels he is not emotionally ready for me to confront him. What should I do?

Response: If your child is currently seeing a professional counselor, we firmly believe you should listen to him or her. Under no circumstances alter how you are dealing with your child unless you discuss it thoroughly with your child's counselor. This book is not a replacement for professional counseling for your child.

Question: I am afraid that if I crack down hard on my twelve-year-old for minor problems, such as staying out too late or not listening to us, I will not have any disciplinary methods left if she really acts bad. What do you have to say about this?

Response: Many parents share your feelings. But experience shows us very clearly that, unless you've set limits on your child's minor problems, by the time he or she engages in major problems (drugs, for example) you may have lost so much control that there will be no means left for you to influence the child's behavior.

5

ASSERTIVE DISCIPLINE PLAN: STEP TWO
Backing Up Your Words with Disciplinary Action

The second step in establishing an Assertive Discipline Plan is to determine how you will respond if your children do not comply with your requests or demands. Backing up your words with action is essential if you want results. For many children, as we stated earlier, "Actions do speak louder than words." In order to assert your influence effectively, often it is necessary to demonstrate your sincerity by reinforcing your verbal requests or demands with appropriate consequences. We are not advocating that you run around your house continually telling your children, "Do what I tell you to do or I will send you to your room." What we are saying, and have said, is that you should determine consequences to use when it is necessary and appropriate to back up your words with actions: "Come home on time or you will choose to be grounded."

When parents are assertive they *promise* rather than *threaten* to back up their verbal requests with actions. A "promise" is a vow of affirmative action. A "threat" is a statement or expression of intention to hurt or punish. When parents are assertive they promise to back up their words with actions because they are aware that providing needed discipline is an affirmative positive action which will benefit their children. When parents are assertive they also demonstrate that to allow their children to engage in inappropriate, self-destructive behavior is a risk to their children's well-being and

71

in the long run is the severest punishment that can be inflicted upon their children.

Even though disciplining children, if done appropriately, is an affirmative action which will benefit the children, we know of no parent—ourselves included—who enjoys laying down the law! No parent likes the stress and discomfort inherent in the disciplinary process. We cannot imagine a parent being elated about finding it necessary to send a child to his or her room or having to ground the child for an extended period of time. We cannot imagine a parent being elated when his or her children say "You're mean" or "That's unfair," cry, or have a tantrum as a direct result of the parent's disciplinary actions. In being assertive, parents recognize that disciplinary limit-setting is an unpleasant, yet essential, responsibility inherent in the role as a loving, caring parent.

GUIDELINES FOR ACTIONS

We have mentioned the need for effective consequences to back up your words with your actions. How do you decide what consequences you will use? Here are the basic guidelines we have found useful in determining the consequences to be used:

You and Your Spouse Must Agree on the Consequences.

Just as you and your spouse have to agree on the behavior you want your children to engage in, you must agree as well on what disciplinary consequences will be utilized. Effective discipline requires teamwork between husband and wife. There is no teamwork if one spouse feels the discipline is too tough or too easy. You and your spouse need to sit down and together determine consequences that would be appropriate and that you could both whole-heartedly support.

The Consequences Must Be Something That the Children Do Not Like but That Is Not Physically or Psychologically Harmful.

Any discipline, to be effective, must be something the children do not particularly enjoy happening. A four- or five-year-old probably will not enjoy being sent to his or her room for ten or fifteen minutes, but typical twelve- or thirteen-year-olds would probably not mind being sent to their rooms, where they would be able to entertain themselves with TV, radio, or cassette players. If you are having trouble thinking of consequences you feel your children would not like, see the examples at the bottom of this section.

The disciplinary consequences should not be enjoyable to children, but, on the other hand, the consequences should not degrade or terrorize them either physically or emotionally. No disciplinary consequence should humiliate or degrade a child in any way. For example, we heard of a six-year-old boy who often wet his pants. His mother became so angry that she would hang the soiled pants on the wall in the family room for all to see. Or there was the father who would make his six-year-old daughter sit in the closet when she misbehaved. Or the parents who forced their children to stand out in the snow for long periods of time when they were disruptive. Do not forget that the goal of discipline is to help your children and to teach them more productive, appropriate ways of action. It is not a means for you to vent your frustrations and hostility upon them.

The most common disciplinary consequences parents utilize successfully include the following:

Separation: The children are separated from you and others into a nonstimulating, "boring" situation such as standing in the corner, going to their room, or the guest room, or sitting on the porch. If you send the children to their own room you may want to remove their favorite toys, games, TV, or tape player to ensure that the consequence is boring, not enjoyable.

Taking away privileges: You suspend the child's privilege to watch TV, play outside, use the telephone, eat snacks, etc.

"Do what I want first": You make your children comply with your request before they can do something they want—"You cannot go outside and play until you clean up."

Grounding: You restrict your children to their yard, house, or room for a specific amount of time.

Physical action: You respond to your children by holding them, physically making them do what you want, or giving them a swat.

In the Appendix, we will provide detailed descriptions of various types of disciplinary consequences you may find useful in planning how to deal with your children.

Whenever Possible, the Consequences Should Be Logically Related to the Misbehavior.

You will teach your children appropriate behavior more quickly when the disciplinary consequences you use are logically related to the misbehavior rather than if you use random punishment.

Your five-year-old does not pick up her toys. The logical consequence would be to take her toys away for one or two days. A random punishment may be prohibiting TV. Your nine-year-old comes home an hour late for dinner. The logical consequence would be that he is not allowed to go out the next day after school to play. A random punishment may be canceling a weekend movie.

You can see that there is a logical relationship between the child's leaving toys out and your taking them away or between the child's coming in late and your forbidding him to go out the next day. Your children can see and understand the relationship between the misbehavior and the consequence as well as you can. On the other hand, there is no connection between leaving toys out and losing TV privileges or between coming home late and having a weekend movie canceled. When the consequences you use make sense to your children, the discipline will not only be more meaningful but it will not cause the anger or resentment that can be aroused by random arbitrary punishment. Here are some additional examples of logical consequences.

BEHAVIOR PROBLEM	LOGICAL CONSEQUENCE
Your ten-year-old damages your tools.	He is not allowed to use your tools for two weeks.
Your fourteen-year-old continually plays the stereo too loud in her room.	You take the stereo out of her room for one week.
Your nine-year-old willfully breaks his brother's toy.	He has to use his allowance to buy his brother another toy.
Your five-year-old splashes water and makes a mess in the bathroom when taking a bath.	She is required to clean up the bathroom.

Plan to Provide the Consequence to the Child as a Choice.

An integral part of backing up your words with actions is to provide your children with a choice. Your limit-setting consequences need to be spelled out to your children so that *they* can make the choice as to whether or not the consequence will occur.

Parent: Adam, I want you to keep your hands to yourself at the dinner table. If you poke or hit your brother you will choose to sit in the corner. It's your choice!

Adam: O.K. (*However, he gradually begins to poke his brother under the table.*)

Parent: Adam, you poked your brother; you have chosen to go sit in the corner for the remainder of dinner.

When you provide your children with the choice as to whether or not the disciplinary consequences will occur, you place the responsibility where it belongs—on the children. The child is one who chooses to poke his brother; thus he is the one who chooses to sit in the corner. When you give your children choices, you are providing them with the opportunity to learn the natural consequences of their inappropriate actions and that they are responsible for their behavior.

• Let's summarize the points we have just made related to determining your disciplinary consequences. Both you and your spouse must agree upon the consequences to be utilized. The consequence should be logically related to the misbehavior and must be something your children do not want to happen. Finally, the consequence must be provided to your children as a choice.

CONSISTENCY

Just as important as planning the consequences you will utilize is planning to utilize them consistently. Often in our workshops we hear parents state, "Nothing will work with those children, I have tried everything—I yell, I scream, I ground them, I even swat them." When we look at a parent's responses to the children's acting up, we typically find that the parents have been inconsistent. Such inconsistency is beautifully illustrated by the following example:

Jack and Margaret were having problems dealing with their eight- and ten-year-olds' continual arguing and fighting. It seemed the two boys were at each other's throats whenever they were alone together. The problem was at its worst after dinner when the boys could not go outside and play. It got to the point where the parents had tried everything from yelling and screaming to taking away TV and grounding.

One night when the boys were particularly disruptive, Jack and Margaret sat down with them and told them, "We have had it. There will be no more arguments or fights. If you choose to argue and fight after dinner, you will be sent to bed immediately. There will be no TV, no snack. This rule is in effect from now on!" Ten minutes later the boys were at it again. The parents, as they had said they would, sent them immediately to bed.

The first night after the parents cracked down, the boys were fine. Jack and Margaret breathed a collective sigh of relief.

The second night, the boys had one argument. The parents responded with their usual yelling, "Cut it out," adding, "Don't make us send you to bed early." They thought about sending the boys to bed as they had said they would, but agreed, "The boys were so much better than before, so why bother?"

The third and fourth nights, the boys had two big arguments and one small one each night. The parents again yelled and threatened to put them to bed early, but did not because they thought that the boys were not as "bad" as they had been.

From the fourth night on, the boys reverted to their usual continual disruptions. Both parents threw up their hands. "Nothing works with those boys. We sent them to bed early; they shaped up for a few days, and now they are at it again, as bad as ever."

It is important to note that sending the boys to bed was in fact an effective disciplinary consequence that did work. We can see that it was effective because it motivated the boys to stop carrying on the next night. If it could stop them for one night, then it could motivate them to stop for a longer period of time. The key, again, is the consistent use of the consequence (sending the boys to bed early). The parents' follow-through efforts did not work because they allowed the boys' fighting to resume on the second, third, fourth, and fifth nights without providing the consequence that they had promised would occur. For the parents to be effective they would not only have had to send the boys to bed on the first night there was an outburst but on each night that they misbehaved, as the parents had promised. In reality, nothing will work unless you, the parent, are prepared to—and do—consistently back up your words with actions when your children's behavior requires you to do so!

You may have to stand your four-year-old in the corner two or three times a day for several days until she realizes you will not accept her whining and complaining.

You may need to have your seven-year-old, before he can go out to play, finish his schoolwork at home three or four times a week for several weeks. He must learn you will not accept his not doing his work at school.

You may have to ground your thirteen-year-old in her room almost daily until she learns she cannot sass and talk back to you.

Once again, the message you send by being consistent is this: I love you too much to allow you to misbehave without my responding.

MONITORING YOUR CHILDREN'S BEHAVIOR

Many of your children's problem behaviors can and will occur when you are not present. The children may act up at school, with a sitter, at a neighbor's, or when they are at home alone. You cannot be truly consistent in your efforts unless you plan ways to *monitor* your children's behavior in order to discipline them if they misbehave even when you are not present. Here are some typical examples of how parents have successfully monitored the behavior of their children.

Telephone Calls: Call on a regular basis to check up on the children's behavior.

> Your nine-year-old is constantly a severe problem in class. You call the teacher or have the teacher call you on a daily basis to report on your child's behavior.

> Your six-year-old refuses to go to bed when the sitter tells her to. You call at bedtime and check up on her.

> Your twelve-year-old is to come home right after school and do her chores. You call her at the appropriate time to make sure she is at home and that her chores are done.

> Your fourteen-year-old says she is going to a party at a friend's and that the friend's parents will chaperone. You call the parents to be sure one or both will be there.

Neighbor's Visits: Have a trusted neighbor stop by and check on your children when you are not home.

> Your children do not do their homework when they are home alone. You have your neighbor come over to make sure it is done.

Your children become wild when they stay with the sitter. You have your neighbor stop by periodically to make sure the children are behaving.

Tape Recordings: You record the behavior of your children on tape so, if necessary, you can hear how they behaved while you were away. This is particularly effective if your children deny that they misbehave when you have been told they do.

Your thirteen-year-old talks back to his math teacher. You have the teacher record the entire class period.

Your seven-year-old will not listen to the babysitter. You have the sitter tape-record their interactions.

Written Notes: You have your children's teacher report to you in writing on their behavior.

Your ten-year-old does not do his homework. You have the teacher send you a note each day on the work that he must finish at home.

By monitoring their behavior you will demonstrate to your children your determination to teach them more appropriate behavior. You will show that you care about how they behave, not only when they are with you but when they are alone or with others.

DISCIPLINE HIERARCHY

Before we finish this chapter we want to present an excellent idea many parents find useful in helping them to structure their disciplinary efforts—a *Discipline Hierarchy*. A Discipline Hierarchy is a particularly effective approach to use if your children engage in the same misbehavior many times per day: for example, if they continually argue, interrupt, fight, or refuse to cooperate.

In a Discipline Hierarchy, your disciplinary consequences are ranked in order of severity. If your children continue to misbehave, they will receive increasingly severe consequences. For example:

> First time your child does not cooperate: Warning that he or she will be disciplined the next time.
>
> Second time your child does not cooperate: Fifteen minutes in his or her room.
>
> Third time your child does not cooperate: Thirty minutes in his or her room.
>
> Fourth time your child does not cooperate: One hour in his or her room.

The Discipline Hierarchy should be simple. It should contain a maximum of three or four consequences. The hierarchy should begin with a minor consequence such as a warning and progress in severity to more serious consequences such as grounding in the child's room for an extended period of time.

Most parents find it useful to keep track of their children's misbehavior by recording each disruption on a piece of paper or a chalkboard placed in a strategic location like a refrigerator or a bulletin board. The first time the child misbehaves the parents write the child's name on a sheet of paper or a chalkboard as a warning. The next time the child breaks a rule, the parent calmly puts a check, red mark, etc. next to the child's name, which indicates that the next consequence has been provided. Each subsequent misbehavior earns an additional check. This record-keeping enables you to be aware at all times of the consequences that your child has earned and of what consequences would next be provided for the child.

In addition, each day your child starts out with a clean slate. That means no matter how many times your children disrupted the previous day, they begin with the first consequence on your plan the first time they disrupt the next day. It is not beneficial to punish your children on Wednesday for the accumulated behavior problems that occurred on Tuesday.

Please note: When you are using the Discipline Hierarchy and your children's behavior is not improving, you may have to make your hierarchy "tougher." Let's say your hierarchy reads as follows:

First time your child argues: Name written on chalkboard; warning that he or she will be disciplined next time.

Second time your child argues: One check next to name; child loses right to watch television the remainder of the day.

Third time your child argues: Two checks; child loses the right to play outside for the remainder of the day.

Fourth time your child argues: Three checks; child is sent to bed right after dinner.

Each day for the past four days your daughter has had two loud arguments with you, and each day you write her name on the chalkboard attached to the refrigerator and take away her TV privileges. What she is revealing by her repeated misbehavior is that she does not really care about the first *two* consequences you are providing her. In order to motivate her to change her behavior, you would need to modify your plan to read that now the first time she argues with you she will not receive a warning or lose TV, but will receive the third consequence—lose the right to go outside and play.

One last point on the Discipline Hierarchy: We do not want you to interpret anything we have said to mean that you *must* utilize a Discipline Hierarchy. We want to state again that a Discipline Hierarchy may prove useful to you if your children consistently engage in the same misbehavior many times per day.

FAMILY EXAMPLE

In the previous chapter in the Family Example, we discussed how the parents, Emily and Steve, began their Assertive Discipline Plan by determining the behavior their children must improve: "Follow directions." In this chapter, we will discuss how the parents determine the disciplinary consequences to be included in their discipline plan.

Emily and Steve thought carefully about the consequences they would utilize to back up their words with actions if their children did not behave. They reviewed the consequences listed in the Appendix. They discussed a number of consequences: taking away allowance, no Little League for Kevin, no dance class for Karen. Either Emily or Steve was uncomfortable with one or the other of the consequences. They finally agreed upon sending their children to their rooms and making them stay there without playing with their toys, cassette player, record player, etc.

Because the children failed so frequently to cooperate, Steve felt that it would be a good idea to set up a Discipline Hierarchy and provide the children increasingly longer periods of separation in their rooms if they continued to misbehave. He came up with the following Discipline Hierarchy for each child. He made Kevin's stronger, for he felt his son was older and thus needed more time in his room for the consequences to be effective.

Karen's Discipline Hierarchy

First time she does not follow directions: Warning.

Second time she does not follow directions: Fifteen minutes in her room without playing with toys or games.

Third time she does not follow directions: Thirty minutes in her room without playing with toys or games.

Fourth time she does not follow directions: One hour in her room without playing with toys or games.

Kevin's Discipline Hierarchy

First time he does not follow directions: Warning.

Second time he does not follow directions: Thirty minutes in his room without games or cassette player.

Third time he does not follow directions: One hour in his room without games or cassette player.

Fourth time he does not follow directions: One hour and a half in his room without games or cassette player.

Emily thought that the Discipline Hierarchies were not "tough" enough. She proposed that the children would also lose the right to TV if they did not cooperate more than one time per day. Steve agreed, so they changed each plan to read that the *second* time a child did not follow directions it would mean time in his or her room *and* no TV for the remainder of the day.

Emily was also concerned about what they should do if the children would not stay in their rooms or played with their toys or cassette player even when they were told not to. They agreed that if the children disregarded either consequence they would be made to stay in their rooms an additional half hour and that the cassette player or toys would be removed from the room.

The last aspect of determining their disciplinary consequences was for Emily and Steve to plan how they would monitor their children's behavior when they, the parents, were not at home. They felt this was necessary because within the last few months Kevin especially had begun to refuse to cooperate when he was left with sitters. He was particularly difficult around bedtime. On several occasions the sitters reported they could not get him into bed until hours past his bedtime.

The parents felt it would be useful to phone the sitter at *Kevin's bedtime*. If he was not in bed they would demand he go to bed, and the following day he would receive the next consequence on his Discipline Hierarchy.

When Emily and Steve had determined what the disciplinary

consequences would be and how they would monitor them, they had completed the second step of their Assertive Discipline Plan for each child.

• In this chapter we have discussed backing up your words with disciplinary action. To summarize, you and your spouse must utilize disciplinary consequences whenever your children do not comply with your requests or demands. Monitor your children's behavior to ensure they do what you want. If your children engage in the same misbehavior many times each day, you may want to use a Discipline Hierarchy.

SOME QUESTIONS PARENTS ASK RELATED TO TOPICS IN THIS CHAPTER

Question: I'm a single parent. How do I find the time or energy to be as consistent as you say is necessary?

Response: We are well aware that being a single parent makes the job of disciplining your children much more difficult. But you still can be consistent; you still can be effective. Stop believing that just because you are a single parent you cannot get your children to behave. You can, and if you follow the guidelines presented in this book, you will be able to.

Question: I always let my child know what will happen if she breaks a rule and what the consequences are that she will choose, but she still blames me and gets upset whenever I discipline her.

Response: You are going to have to let the child know that she is the one who chooses to be disciplined because she misbehaves. Some children continue to get upset and try to manipulate you by blaming you. Don't listen to them.

Question: I think grounding my children at home punishes me more than them. Having them around the house is sometimes just too much for me to handle. What do you suggest?

Response: Any consequence that you use with your children, you must be comfortable with. If you are not comfortable grounding your children, please do not use that as a consequence when your children misbehave. Come up with some other consequence (taking away a privilege, etc.) that you feel would best meet your needs.

Question: When my kids misbehave, I take away TV. The problem I have, though, is that the kids wander around the house and "bug" me, complaining that they have nothing to do. What do you suggest?

Response: If, when you take TV away from your children, they begin to bother you, we would recommend that you tell your children very clearly that unless they find something to do, you may have to put them in their rooms so that they will stop bothering you. Many children try to punish the parents for taking TV away by harassing them. Don't allow this.

Question: My children are often late for school because they are watching TV and do not get ready in time. I have thus set up a plan that they can not watch TV until they are dressed in the morning. The problem is, they still watch TV. What can I do?

Response: It will be necessary for you to monitor your children more closely in the morning to make sure they get dressed without watching TV. You may also want to consider unplugging the TV in the morning so the children cannot watch it.

Question: Our son is in constant trouble at school. We have grounded him, taken away TV, and nothing works. All he cares about is Little League. I hate to take that away from him. How do you feel about this?

Response: What is more important to you—your child's behaving at school or his taking part in Little League? Your child may have to know that he will choose to miss Little League if he disrupts at school. Without that reality hanging over his head, he may not accept that you do mean business.

Question: We often have problems with our children's behavior when we go out to eat at a restaurant. Do you have any suggestions?

Response: Here is an idea one father we worked with presented that proved highly effective. His children were continuously disruptive whenever they went out to eat. It was rare that a meal at a restaurant wasn't punctuated with yelling and screaming by all the children. The father had tried everything he could think of, to no avail. Finally he came up with the following plan. He told the children, "If any one of you disrupts when we go out to the restaurant tonight we will all come home and whoever disrupted will go right to bed." Soon after they arrived at the restaurant his youngest son began to be disruptive. The father canceled the order with the waitress, put all the kids in the car, and drove home. His son was escorted immediately to bed. Not only was his son unhappy about going to bed early, he had to bear the brunt of brothers and sisters being unhappy that they were deprived of a meal at their favorite restaurant. The father had to demonstrate his concern by using such a strong consequence only once.

Question: My teenager continually lies to me about where she is. I have tried everything. Do you have any ideas about what I can do?

Response: We worked with a father who had the same problem with his daughter. Nothing he tried worked until he told his daughter he would allow her to go out—on one condition. Every hour or two she must call him and report where she was. Periodically, he would have her stay at the location and he would drive there to make sure she was where she had told him she was. The father did not like doing this. The daughter liked it even less. However, after a few weeks this method produced results, and the father was able to monitor her behavior effectively and ensure she was telling the truth. *Please note:* This is a strong approach to dealing with a teenager and should be used only when all else has failed.

6

ASSERTIVE DISCIPLINE PLAN: STEP THREE
How to Reinforce
Your Children
When They Do Behave

In the last chapter we discussed planning how you will respond when your children do not behave. Just as important is planning how you will respond when your children do behave. One of the keys to effective discipline is knowing how to react successfully to your children's appropriate behavior.

> You have had trouble with your child's talking back. How do you respond when he is cooperative?
> Your children continually argue and fight with each other. How do you respond when they play quietly?
> Your child is a constant problem at school. How do you respond when you get a good report from her teacher?

Unfortunately, most parents do not take charge and respond in an assertive "I like that" manner when their children do behave. The majority of parents respond in a passive, nonassertive manner which does not motivate the children to continue their appropriate behavior.

When your children behave you must be prepared to reinforce their behavior. By *reinforce*, we mean responding in a manner which, through your words and actions, demonstrates your approval and appreciation of your child's positive behavior. Your reinforcement may take various forms.

Praise: Jesse, I like the way you cleaned up your toys.

Special Privileges: Justin, you played so nicely with your brother that you may stay up one hour later.

Material reward: Gabe and Josh, you kids have been so cooperative that you may go to McDonald's for lunch.

Why is reinforcement so critical? When you assertively reinforce your children's appropriate behavior you will encourage them to continue the behavior you want and the behavior that is in their own best interests. Your children will know that you like the behavior that you reinforce and they will be more likely to continue this behavior than if you did not reinforce it. Let's elaborate on how you can reinforce your children's behavior.

PRAISE – THE BEST REINFORCER

Your children's emotional well-being and self-confidence are directly related to the feedback they receive from you. The more positive your responses, the better they can and will feel. All too often though, parents spend most of their time telling their children, "Don't do that," "That's wrong," "I don't like that," rather than focusing on what they do like, "Hey, good job," "Thanks for doing that," "Super."

One of the best ways to communicate your love and concern to your children is to permeate your relationship with your positive feedback. Don't take their "good behavior" for granted. Let your children know how much you appreciate it when they behave.

Mother to Child: Jamie, I sure had a nice day with you. Your helpfulness has been a real pleasure. I want to make sure Dad knows this when he comes home.

Mother to Father (in child's presence): I had such a nice day with Jamie. I was so proud of her cooperation today.

Father to Child: I really like getting such good reports from Mom about you. I feel you are really special. *(Father hugs child.)*

Effective parents are aware of the enormous impact their praise can have and will utilize it not only to build their children's self-esteem, but to help them learn appropriate behavior. Praise is the most useful, positive reinforcer you possess.

When praising your children, keep the following ideas in mind.

Tell them, specifically, what they are doing, or have done, that you like. "I really do appreciate how quietly you are sitting in the back seat, Natalie," rather than making a vague comment such as, "You are a good girl, Natalie."

When you deliver your verbal praise be sure to walk up to your children, look them in the eye, and, if appropriate, give them a warm pat on the shoulder in order to increase the impact of your message.

When you praise your children watch out for hostile, sarcastic comments. The quickest way to turn your children off is to couple your positive comments with negative "hooks": "I like the way you cleaned up today. It's about time." "Thank you for helping your sister. I expect you to do the same tomorrow." "You were so good today. I sure like it, but I can't believe you acted so nice." These digs are poorly veiled hostilities on the part of frustrated parents.

Finally, do not overuse praise. If you constantly tell your children "I like . . ." basically everything they do, they will soon tire of your comments. Your children will pick up that you are on a new "kick" and are not sincere in what you are saying.

Hand-in-hand with verbal praise go nonverbal responses. A hug can mean as much or more than countless "I like that's." A smile, a wink, a pat on the shoulder—all communicate your positive support and recognition of your children's behavior.

Let's quickly summarize the points we have just made. Praise is critical to the well-being of your children. Be sure to praise your children when they do what you want. Make sure your praise is sincere. Finally, along with your praise don't hesitate to use hugs, etc.

BACKING UP PRAISE WITH POSITIVE CONSEQUENCES

Some children may not be sufficiently motivated by your praise to improve their behavior quickly. This can be common with school-age children. If your children are insufficiently motivated, it would be well worth it to you and your children to combine your praise with additional motivators, whether they are *special privileges* or *material rewards*.

We are aware that many parents are reluctant to reward their children with anything but praise because they are afraid that their children will become used to a pattern of behaving only if they get some reward. For example:

> I will not clean up my room unless you promise to read a story.
> What will you give me for doing the dishes?

Please don't forget that even when using rewards you are still the boss! Your children do not decide what rewards they will receive for behaving—you do. If your children want to get into a power struggle with you and try to extort rewards by threat of misbehavior, do not tolerate it. Deliver the following message to your children: "I can not tolerate your demanding rewards."

Now that we have addressed this realistic concern we want to present two excellent approaches parents have found successful in helping them reinforce their children. We call these ideas Positive Contracts and Marble Mania.

POSITIVE CONTRACTS

First we will discuss Positive Contracts. A Positive Contract is basically an agreement between you and your children that states: "When you do what I want, in return I will provide you something you want."

> When you do your chores, I will give you an allowance.
> When you spend all day without arguing or talking back, I will give you a point. When you have five points, you and I will do a project in my workshop.

A Positive Contract is a helpful way to structure your reinforcement and positive support. When our son was young we used a positive contract with him to help teach him to get ready for school on his own. We told him that if he got up, washed, and dressed by himself, we would give him a "happy face." When he got three happy faces he could get a "grab" from our "grab bag." In the grab bag we included small toys, sugarless gum, and other small surprises. Our son loved the plan. Within a short time he learned to get ready for school with no hassles.

You can get the same results with your children. Here are some basic guidelines on making and utilizing a Positive Contract with your children.

The contract must include what you want your child to do and what you will allow him or her to earn. You need to determine the specific behaviors you want to reinforce and what reward you will provide your children. Once again, a word of warning: Make sure the reward is not something that is too expensive or time-consuming to provide, such as a large toy or a trip.

The contract must be designed so that your children can earn the reward in an appropriate amount of time. *Please note:* Most children simply cannot comprehend or be motivated effectively by long-range rewards. You need to plan your contract so that your children will be able to earn the positive consequences in a short period of time. The younger the child, the more quickly he or she needs to earn the consequence.

Three- to four-year-olds earn the reward within maximum one day.

Five- to eight-year-olds earn the reward within maximum one week.

Nine- to thirteen-year-olds earn the reward within maximum two weeks.

Thirteen-year-olds and older earn the reward within maximum four weeks.

The contract should be in effect for a specific period of time. The contract should specify that the agreement will last for one week, two weeks, a month. When the time limit on the contract is over, determine if it would be helpful to draw up a new one. Decide if you want to change the consequences and ask the child if he or she wants something different as a reward. You will also want to decide if you want the child to engage in more positive behavior to earn the reward. For example, if it took ten points to earn time with you, maybe under this contract it would take fifteen or twenty points, or if the child needed to cooperate for one hour to earn a point, it would now take two hours.

To further assist you in developing a contract with your child or children, here are some examples of typical contracts parents have utilized:

Four-year-old who consistently interrupts mom when she is on the phone.

For each time that I am on the phone and you do not interrupt me, you will earn a jellybean.

Seven-year-old who teases his sister.

For every hour that you spend without calling your sister a name, you will get a chip. When you have twenty chips, you and I will make a hand puppet.

Twelve-year-old who is a behavior problem at school and who does not do her homework:

For every day that you follow directions in class and do your homework without my having to tell you, you will earn a point. When you earn ten points, you may have extra money to go to the video arcade.

Let's go over what we have just discussed. A positive contract can be an excellent way to reinforce your children. Contracts must be carefully planned to specify what you want your children to do and what reward they can earn quickly if they do comply.

MARBLE MANIA

The second positive idea you may find useful is what we call "Marble Mania." This is designed to be utilized when you have more than one child who is misbehaving. Marble Mania is the most exciting, useful, and fun way we have ever found to motivate children four years old and older to shape up. Here's how Marble Mania works. When any of your children behave as you have told them to, let them know you like it, and put a marble in a jar: "Brandon, I really like how you have cooperated. You have earned a marble for that."

When the children fill the jar or reach a predetermined goal, such as fifty, one hundred, or two hundred marbles, *all* of the children in the family earn the reward they want. (If you do not want to use marbles, you can give the children a point on a chart, a star, sticker, or a chip.) The reward may be the same for all the children, or each child may be provided a personalized reward. For example:

When you earn a hundred marbles, we will take all of you to see the new *Star Wars* movie.

When you earn a hundred marbles, Emmy Lou will get to go shopping for clothes with Mom, and Kris will earn the right to go bowling with a friend.

In addition, the children should be provided "bonus" marbles for each day they all go without misbehaving.

For each day that all of you children go without misbehaving, we will put ten bonus marbles in the jar.

The foundation of the tremendous success for a family reward system such as Marble Mania is the *peer pressure* that is fostered. By allowing all your children to earn something they want, they will be encouraged to motivate their siblings to be "good" in order to earn the reward as quickly as possible. You will hear the children imploring one another:

Stop bugging Mom! The less you carry on, the more marbles we will get, and the sooner we will both get what we want.

We have got to cut out our arguing. The less we fight, the more marbles Mom and Dad put in the jar. I don't know about you, but I want that prize!

Look, quit messing up! We can get ten extra marbles if we

both go for the entire day without getting into trouble. So dog-gone it, listen to Mom and the sitter!

Such peer pressure results in your children effectively motivating each other and consequently taking a great deal of pressure off you and your spouse. The more your children are motivated to get along with each other and to stop their brother or sister from acting up, the easier it will be for you.

Here are some concepts to ensure the success of your Marble Mania plan. First, make sure your children earn a large number of marbles each day. Approximately once per hour to hour and a half, stop what you are doing and reward each child who has behaved as you have told him or her to by putting another marble in the jar. Be sure to let your children know what you are doing: "Steven, Bret, good job playing cooperatively. That's another marble for each of you."

If you need help remembering to reinforce your children, set your kitchen timer to ring in an hour or an hour and a half. When it rings give your children marbles if they have behaved. To make sure each child is being equally reinforced, you can use a different color marble for each child.

Never remove marbles from the jar when the children misbehave. If the children have earned the marbles, they deserve to keep them. Just as you should never take away a negative consequence because the children have improved their behavior, do not take away marbles because the children have misbehaved. We have found that some parents are so negative that by the end of the day they have taken away so many marbles the children actually end up "owing" the parents marbles.

At the end of each day, count the marbles in the jar and indicate the number to the children: "Kids, you have earned sixty-eight marbles. When you earn thirty-two more, you will have a hundred altogether and you will get your reward."

By counting up the number of marbles in the jar at the end of the day, you will also help yourself keep track of how positive you have been with your children. If the total number of marbles in the jar approximates one marble per child every hour or hour and a half, you have been doing an excellent job praising your children's appropriate behavior.

We want to make one last point regarding Positive Contracts and Marble Mania. You may be concerned that you are going to have to continually devise new contracts or Marble Mania programs to motivate your children to behave. This will not be the case. When you couple your positive reinforcement efforts with firm consistent disciplinary consequences, you will find you will need to utilize these positive programs only a few times before your children shape up and no longer require additional motivation.

HOW TO REINFORCE YOUR CHILDREN ASSERTIVELY

Now let's look at how you can go about assertively reinforcing your children's behavior, whether you use praise or back your words up with special rewards. Here are some basic guidelines we have found it necessary to follow.

You and Your Spouse Must Agree upon and Be Comfortable with the Method of Reinforcements.

What will you do when your children behave? Will you praise them? Will you provide them privileges such as extra time with you, staying up later, or having a friend sleep over? Will you provide them with material rewards such as special treats, toys, or money? You and your spouse must agree upon the positive responses with which you are both comfortable. The reinforcement will not be effective if one parent rewards appropriate behavior with praise and extra privileges while the other parent ignores the behavior.

You and Your Spouse Must Determine the Specific Behavior You Want to Reinforce.

Just telling your children "I like . . ." everything they do, or taking them to the park, or giving them extra allowance will not help them to shape up. Review the specific problems you are planning to work on from Step One. Now determine the behavior you want from them. For instance, the appropriate behavior that you desire if your child is not cooperating is that the child follow your directions. If your child is arguing with his sister, the appropriate behavior you want is that he cooperate with his sister. If your child is coming home late, the appropriate behavior you desire is that she come home on time. See the Appendix for more examples.

Your Reinforcing Response Must Be Something Your Children Want.

Ask yourself, what would my children like to earn? In order that your positive response motivate your children to continue the behavior you desire, the reward must be something they need or would like to have. Some children will "walk on water" simply for your praise. Other children desire sharing activities with you. Some would be motivated by a visit to a video arcade, some by staying out late at night.

. If you are not sure what rewards would most motivate your children, see the Appendix for a questionnaire to give them.

Let's summarize the points we have just made related to determining how you will reinforce your children when they behave. You and your spouse must agree upon the consequences you will use. The consequences must be something that your children want and that is provided to them when they do what you have asked.

FAMILY EXAMPLE

In the previous chapter we discussed in the Family Example how the parents, Emily and Steve, determined the disciplinary consequences to use in their Assertive Discipline Plan. We are now going to show how the parents determined the positive consequences to be included in their plan.

The parents, especially Steve, recognized that they were not reinforcing their children in an assertive manner when they did cooperate. Like many parents, they felt their children should cooperate because it was the "right" thing for children to do.

Steve was comfortable with and recognized the need for praising the children when they did cooperate. He was, however, reluctant to provide them rewards for behaving. Emily, on the other hand, felt rewards would prove useful in motivating the children to improve their behavior more quickly. She loved the idea of putting marbles in the jar when the children cooperated. She thought this was unlike anything they had tried with the children before and it might just prove novel enough to excite them. Under Emily's prodding, Steve agreed to try a marble program one time.

The next thing the parents had to discuss was the rewards their children would earn in the marble program. Both were sure that Karen would be highly motivated by the opportunity to earn an additional dance lesson. They were not sure, though, about Kevin. They sat down with Kevin and used the reward survey included in the Appendix of this book to determine what would motivate him. All Kevin wanted to know was "Why are you asking me these questions?" The parents responded, "We want to know better the kinds of things you like to do." When they had finished the questionnaire it was clear Kevin most wanted to earn a trip to the video arcade with his dad.

The parents realized that the success of the marble program for the children would be based on their earning a large number of marbles per day and earning the reward quickly, within about one week. They felt sure that if the kids had to wait much beyond a week, they would probably lose interest and not be motivated.

After some quick thinking, the parents figured out that the children were at home or with them approximately five hours per school day and six hours on the weekends. Each child was with them approximately thirty to forty hours per week. The parents felt they should provide each child a marble for every hour he or she cooperated; thus a reasonable goal for the children would be for them to earn their reward when there was a total of seventy marbles in the jar.

Once the parents had determined the consequences they would utilize to reinforce their children's behavior, they had completed Step Three of their Assertive Discipline Plan.

Before we finish this chapter we want to address this important question many parents ask. If positive reinforcement is so necessary, why don't more parents utilize it in a consistent, effective manner? First, we think that so many parents put so much time and energy into hassling with their children when the children are acting up that they lose track of the need to respond to them when they are behaving. Also, many parents honestly believe the only way to get their children to shape up is to discipline them continually when they get out of line.

Second—and most significant—many, if not most, parents feel that their children are "just supposed to be good." They think that there should be no need to praise or reward children for acting as they should and that such praise and rewards are basically nothing more than "bribery." This misguided theory is nonsense. *Bribery* is defined as paying or rewarding an individual for performing some form of illegal or immoral act. Since when is cooperating, doing well in school, taking care of responsibilities, or getting along with other family members illegal or immoral?

Finally, the consistent use of reinforcements will make managing your children's behavior a great deal easier. If you feel that the only way to get your children to behave is to be on their backs and focus only on their problem behavior, a real strain can be placed on your relationship with them. Disciplining children is hard work and not enjoyable for any party involved. The more you support and reinforce your children's appropriate behavior, the less time and energy you will have to spend on disciplining them. We are asking: Would you prefer to put your energy into telling your children that you like the way they are behaving and *possibly* providing them extra privileges or rewards for their positive behavior? Or would you rather deal with the stress and strain of consistently demanding that they "stop" what they are doing, putting them in their rooms, grounding them, or taking away privileges? The answer is obvious.

• In this chapter we have discussed how to reinforce your children when they do behave. Here are the points we want you to remember: It is just as important to plan how you will reinforce your children when they do behave as when they do not. You and your spouse must agree on how to positively reinforce them. While praise is the key to reinforcement, Positive Contracts and Marble Mania may be useful aids.

SOME QUESTIONS PARENTS ASK RELATED TO TOPICS IN THIS CHAPTER

Question: I'm a single parent who works. How can I find the time to reinforce my children's good behavior as needed?

Response: We admit it is more difficult to give your children positive attention being a single parent who works, but it still can be done. You will need to set aside time each day where you can focus on the positive aspects of your children's behavior. The effort will be well worth it.

Question: We really believe in praising our children for everything they do right. But lately, the more we praise them, the more they act up. What are we doing wrong?

Response: Two things. First, your children probably are being overpraised by you. If you go around your house saying, "I like . . ." everything your children do, after a while praise will lose all its meaning for your children. Second, how about setting some limits when your children misbehave? Don't forget, you must balance your positive responses with appropriate limits.

Question: My parents were not big on praising us when we were good and I grew up O.K. Why do I really need to be different with my kids?

Response: Experience has taught us that the more positive you are with your children, the easier it will be to get them to behave. Your parents may not have needed to utilize reinforcement with you and your brothers and sisters, but times are different. If you choose not to utilize reinforcement, be aware that you are choosing to make it more difficult to get your children to behave.

Question: When we ask our children what they would like to earn by their good behavior, all they come up with are toys that are too expensive for us to buy. What do you suggest?

Response: You need to let your children know you cannot afford such expensive rewards and that you are willing to consider cheaper alternatives. You should go through the reinforcement questions in the Appendix and select alternatives your children would want. Don't be intimidated into providing your children rewards you are not comfortable utilizing.

Question: So many of the ideas sound fine for little kids. How can I use Assertive Discipline with my teenagers?

Response: From our experience with thousands of parents we can tell you Assertive Discipline will work just as well with your teenagers as with your younger children. We want to make one point clear: You must develop an Assertive Discipline Plan that includes consequences you feel are appropriate for your teenagers. There is no way that some of the ideas we have presented would work with teenagers; they are designed to be used with younger children. It is up to you, the parent, to adapt the ideas we have presented in a manner that will enable you to increase your ability to deal with your own children, whether teenage or younger.

7

ASSERTIVE DISCIPLINE PLAN: STEP FOUR
Laying Down the Law

Now it is time to put your Assertive Discipline Plan into action. Your plan at this point must include the behavior you expect your children to change and the consequences you will provide if they do, or do not, behave as you demand. The first step in putting your plan into action is to meet with your children and lay down the law. In this no-nonsense talk you will need to reassert your parental authority in relation to your children's misbehavior. You must demand that your children change their problem behavior. You must send your children the following bottom-line message: "There is no way I am going to tolerate your misbehavior. You can behave, and I care too much about you to allow you to continue such problem behavior!"

GUIDELINES FOR PRESENTING THE PLAN

Here are some basic guidelines to help you effectively present your Assertive Discipline Plan to your child.

Meet with Your Child Only When He or She Is Calm.

To increase the probability that your child will listen to you, confront him or her when he or she is calm. Do not try to talk to your child right after a major fight, when your child or you are upset.

No Siblings Should Be Present When You Meet with the Child.

If only one of your children misbehaved you do not need his or her sibling chiming in and making a scene during your discussion. (If you are having problems with two or more children you can meet with them at the same time.)

Make Sure There Will Be No Distractions When You Meet with Your Child.

Turn off the TV, and stereo, take the phone off the hook, and tell your other children to stay out of the room so you will not be interrupted with your child.

Both Parents Should State Their Demand.

In order to maximize the impact of the conversation, both parents should look the child in the eye and calmly and firmly state the demand to the child.

> **Mother:** Brian, I will not tolerate your wandering around the neighborhood and getting into trouble after school. You must come home right after school and do your homework and chores.
>
> **Father:** I agree with your mom. You have gotten into too much trouble after school. You will come home right after school and get your schoolwork and chores done immediately.

State the Consequence That Will Occur if Your Child Chooses Not to Comply with Your Demands.*

Clearly lay out what your child will choose to happen.

> Brian, if you do not come home straight from school and do your schoolwork and chores, you will be grounded for the remainder of the day at home with no television. And Brian, if that does not work, we are prepared to ground you in your room for the entire day if you do not obey us!

Tell the Child How You Will Monitor His or Her Behavior.

Your child must know you will, on a regular basis, check up to see if he or she is behaving appropriately, even when you are not present.

> We will call you every day at 3:30 to see that you are home. When we get home from work, we will check to see that your chores and homework are finished. If you are not home when we call, or your work or chores are not done, you will be immediately grounded with no TV.

Post Your Assertive Discipline Plans for All to See.

As soon as you have finished discussing your discipline plan with your child, post a copy of the plan in a prominent location, such as on the refrigerator. This act will add additional impact to your verbal statements. In addition, the posted copy of the plan will serve as

---

* It is not appropriate, when "laying down the law," to discuss positive reinforcement for good behavior. Discuss it at a later time when your children's behavior is under control.

a reminder to your children that you do mean business and a reminder to you that you need to consistently follow through. On each sheet of paper you should write the child's name, the behaviors you have demanded that he or she do, and what will happen if he or she does not comply.

Brian will do his chores and homework right after school. If he chooses not to, he will be grounded with no TV.

If you are using a Discipline Hierarchy, you can list the hierarchy of consequences. For example:

Deborah will follow directions immediately.

If she chooses not to:

The first time: Her name will be written on the chalkboard as a "warning."

The second time: She will receive a check and will be sent to the guest room for ten minutes.

The third time: Two checks and she will be sent to the guest room for twenty minutes and cannot watch TV for the remainder of the day.

The fourth time: Three checks and she will be sent to the guest room for thirty minutes and will go to bed early.

The chalkboard or the piece of paper you use for record-keeping should be placed right next to the Assertive Discipline Plan. One last point on this topic: If your children are too young to read, you may want to make stick-figure drawings to explain your rules and consequences.

Let's review the keys to presenting your Assertive Discipline Plan to your children. You should sit down with your children when they are calm and there will be no distractions. Both you and your spouse must direct your children to do what you want, and explain what will happen if they don't. Finally, post a copy of what you will do for all to see.

CHILDREN'S MANIPULATIONS AND HOW TO DEAL WITH THEM

When you lay down the law to your children it is not uncommon for them to get angry, cry, beg forgiveness, or accuse you of unfairly picking on them. These responses are often utilized by children in an attempt to manipulate their parents into backing down from their limit-setting stance. From our experience many parents can initially state their wants clearly and firmly to their children, but quickly get sidetracked by their children's emotional responses.

> **Father:** Ken, I will not tolerate your fighting. You will not fight with your brother.
>
> **Ken:** It's not my fault. He always starts it.
>
> **Father:** That's not true. You start the fights.
>
> **Ken:** You know you really don't like me. You always pick on me just like everybody else does.
>
> **Father:** Ken, come on. I love you. You're my son! Why do you always feel that everyone picks on you
>
> **Ken:** I feel you pick on me because you are always on my case.
>
> **Father:** Ken, I want to believe you, but it's hard. You get into so many fights. Look, to show you I want to believe you I'll give you another chance.

In this example, you can see how Ken was able to manipulate

and sidetrack his father. His father did not stick to his demand, "You will not fight with your brother." He ended up dealing with Ken's sidetracking responses, "You don't really like me. You always pick on me." When children can manipulate their parents like this, they in effect take control of the conversation, thus preventing the parent from setting the necessary limits.

We have found an effective way to help parents to persist in making their requests or demands known to their children and avoid being manipulated by them. It is called the *broken record*. The broken record gets its name from the way that, when it is utilized, you sound like a broken or stuck record that keeps repeating the same thing over and over and over. . . . When you learn to speak as if you were a broken record, you will be capable of expressing your wants and needs and be able to ignore the sidetracking manipulations of your children. Back to the example of Ken:

> **Father** (with eye contact, hand on shoulder): Ken, you will stop fighting with your brother.
>
> **Ken:** It's not my fault. He picks on me.
>
> **Father** (firmly): That's not the point. You will stop fighting with your brother. (*Broken record*)
>
> **Ken:** You're just picking on me. I'll do what I want!
>
> **Father** (calmly): Ken, you will stop fighting. You have a choice: You will stop fighting or you will be grounded until bedtime. (*Broken record*)
>
> **Ken:** Wow, you just hate me. You're on my case like everybody else is.
>
> **Father** (calmly): Ken, it's your choice. If you choose to fight with your brother, you choose to be grounded until bedtime.

In this interchange, the father simply kept repeating in the "broken-record" method that which he wanted from the child, and the father would not become sidetracked by Ken's responses. The father maintained control of the interaction with the child.

In utilizing a "broken record" you first need to determine what you want from the conversation with the child: e.g., "I want Ken to stop fighting with his brother." This becomes your statement of want and is the point of your conversation. You can preface your statement of want with, "That's not the point. I want you to stop fighting with your brother," or, "I understand, but I want you to stop fighting with your brother." No matter what manipulative responses your child presents, if you respond each time with your statement of want—"That's not the point, I want you to . . . ," or, "I understand, but I want you to. . . . ,"—your statement will be more effective. Also, when delivering your statement of want always remember to utilize appropriate eye contact, gestures, child's name, and touch to add impact to your message.

In most instances, from our experience, when using a broken-record response you will need to repeat your statement of want to your children a maximum of three times and then state the consequences you will provide them if they do not behave.

When utilizing a broken-record response, please remain as calm as possible no matter how your children try to provoke you. We know you may be tempted to argue or even "throttle" your children. Don't scream or yell your demands at them. Verbalize your wants in as firm and calm a tone of voice as possible. Many children will do anything to provoke, upset, or hook you, for they have learned that the more upset their parents become, the easier it is to manipulate or sidetrack them. Don't forget, it takes two people to have a "fight." If you are unwilling to engage in a "fight" with your children, it will make it much more difficult for them to "create a scene" with you.

The benefit of the broken-record response is that it will help you to remain calm and maintain the focus of your wants and needs, rather than being diverted by your children's attempted manipulation. It will also enable you to respond in a manner that your children aren't accustomed to. Children are used to parents being sidetracked by their verbal manipulations, and parents should become aware of typical manipulations that your children may attempt with you. In the following examples note how parents typically ineffectively respond to the manipulations and finally, how they can respond more effectively.

Belligerence

Many older children have learned that their anger can be very effective in "hooking" their parents and thus sidetracking them from being the boss. Here's a prime example of how a child can do this.

> **Mother:** Matt, I will not put up with your refusing to clean your room. You will clean your room now. (*Statement of want*)
>
> **Matt:** I don't give a darn what you say. You can't make me!
>
> **Mother** (fuming): Don't you talk to me that way. Who do you think you are?
>
> **Matt** (angrily): Who do you think you are?
>
> **Mother** (yelling): Listen, young man. I'm not going to take this from you.
>
> **Matt** (screaming): I don't care what you do.
>
> **Mother** (yelling): You are disgusting. You'll be sorry for what you're saying. I won't tolerate anyone's talking to me this way. You get out of here!

The mother obviously allowed Matt's anger to "hook" her. She was responding to Matt's hostility rather than persisting that he clean his room. A more effective response would be as follows:

> **Mother:** Matt, I will not put up with your refusing to clean your room. I want you to clean your room now! (*Statement of want*)

Matt: I don't give a darn what you say. You can't make me. Period.

Mother (calmly, firmly): Matt, I want you to clean your room or you will choose to stay home. (*Broken record*)

Matt: If you want the room cleaned, you do it!

Mother (calmly): Matt, I want you to clean your room or you will choose to stay home. (*Broken record*)

Crying

No one likes to see their children cry. No one likes to feel they made their children upset. Some children quickly learn that if they get upset and cry their parents will feel guilty and stop placing demands on them. Observe how a child can sidetrack her mother, who attempts to deal meaningfully with the child's disruptive behavior in the car.

Mother: Carol, I want you to stop yelling and throwing things when I'm driving. (*Statement of want*)

Carol (beginning to cry): But I didn't do anything.

Mother: Now come on, Carol, no need to get so upset. You don't have to cry every time I talk to you.

Carol (sobbing): I didn't do anything.

Mother: Carol, come on, it's O.K. I'm not angry with you. Just calm down. Take this tissue and blow your nose. We can talk about this when you calm down. You're just having another rough day.

You can see how the parent quickly got sidetracked. A more effective response would be as follows:

Mother: I want you to stop yelling and throwing things when I'm driving. (*Statement of want*)

Carol (beginning to cry loudly): But I didn't do anything.

Mother (firmly): That's not the point. I want you to stop yelling and throwing things. (*Broken record*)

Carol (sobbing): But I didn't do anything.

Mother (calmly): I understand, Carol. You have a choice. Stop yelling and throwing things when I'm driving or I will stop the car and you will have to sit in the front seat away from your friends. (*Broken record*)

"I'm Sorry, Give Me Another Chance."

Some children quickly apologize for their misbehavior and make heartfelt promises never to do it again. They have learned that their "sincere" apologies will many times sidetrack their parents. Here is an excellent example of this.

Father: Suzanne, I will not put up with your leaving a mess every time you paint. Please clean up after yourself. (*Statement of want*)

Suzanne: I'm really sorry, Dad. Please forgive me.

Father: That's what you always say.

Suzanne: I know I've been wrong. I said I'm really sorry."

Father: You promised last week to be good, and yet you made a mess again today.

Suzanne: Dad, I've been really tired lately. I mean it this time. I'll be good, I swear I will.

Father: O.K., Suzanne, one last chance. From now on I want some real effort out of you.

Once again, the parent did not persist with his requests to the child. The child was able to sidetrack her father with promises and apologies. The father truly did not want apologies; he wanted the child to stop making a mess. A more effective response could be as follows:

> **Father:** Suzanne, I will not put up with your leaving a mess every time you paint. Please clean up after yourself! (*Statement of want*)
>
> **Suzanne:** I'm sorry, Dad. Please forgive me.
>
> **Father:** That's not the point. Please clean up after yourself. (*Broken record*)
>
> **Suzanne:** I've really been tired lately. I'm sorry.
>
> **Father** (firmly): I understand, but please clean up after yourself. (*Broken record*)
>
> **Suzanne:** I hear what you are saying. I will clean up after myself right now.

In each of the previous examples, when the parents responded in an assertive manner they did not become sidetracked or "hooked" by the children's anger, tears, or promises. They were able to maintain the focus on their wants and persisted in stating them calmly and firmly.

The "I Don't Care" Child

There is one other type of manipulation that children engage in when you lay down the law. This differs from the highly emotional variety we have just discussed and in many ways is more difficult for parents to handle. We call this manipulation "I don't care." Here's how children use this manipulation. When you tell your children they must behave and you promise to discipline them if they don't, they typically respond with a "So what—who cares?" Such a blasé response is difficult to deal with, since you are probably accustomed to your children giving you a frightened, upset, or distressed look when you tell them you will send them to their room, take away TV, or ground them.

If you are like most parents, when your child says to you, "So what, I don't care if you do that," you get a sinking feeling and say to yourself, "What am I going to do? Nothing works with that child! NOT TRUE! The "I don't care" child is manipulating you. These children have learned that this kind of blasé response often sidetracks their parents from dealing with them effectively. "I don't care" children do not require a broken-record response; They need you to do as these parents did.

Todd was a twelve-year-old who continually sassed his parents and refused to cooperate with them. When his parents confronted him and told him, "We will not tolerate your talking back, and, if you do, we will have you grounded in your room, and we will remove your cassette player and radio while you stay there." His response was simply to grin and say, "So what—who cares what you say?" He was so cocky he added, "Would you like me to go to my room now? It is fine with me."

In the past, his parents would have thrown up their hands in frustration in response to his, "I don't care" attitude. This time, though, they followed through. They stated, "Yes, we want you to go to your room for one hour. If you talk back again or do not cooperate you will stay in your room for two hours, and if that does not work, you will stay in your room for an entire day. All you may do when you are in the room is your schoolwork and you may leave only to eat and to go to the bathroom."

Todd stayed in his room long after the first hour that grounding was over. He finally came out for lunch and quickly began to hassle his mother about the food she had served. "I am sick of this 'crud' you always make. I don't care what you want—I won't eat this food." His mother calmly stated, "You do not talk to me that way. You have chosen to go to your room for three hours." "Bye," said Todd, and away he went to his room, loudly slamming the door behind him. When his three hours were up he came out stating, "I like staying in my room better than anywhere in this house." Again his parents did not respond to his "I don't care" attitude.

There were no problems until dinner when Todd refused to clear away his dishes. His father told him in a matter-of-fact manner, "You have chosen to stay in your room until the same time tomorrow," and sent him off.

The next day when Todd got up, he came out to watch an early football game on TV. His father interrupted him and told him he was still grounded until dinner. Todd got a blank look on his face and exclaimed, "What! I messed up last night—I don't have to stay in my room all day do I?" "Yes," his father said. Todd's face dropped. "That's not fair. I'm sorry I said those things. I'll never talk to you that way again." "I hope not," said his father "but you chose to be grounded today, and you will be." In the middle of the afternoon Todd again began to clamor and apologize in an attempt to come out, but again his parents held firm.

When Todd finally came out, he was very subdued. "I can't believe you made me stay there all day." His mother looked at him and said, "We did not enjoy doing it, Todd, but we can't allow you to talk disrespectfully to us, and we are prepared to send you back to that room again if your actions warrant it."

Your children may not care if you send them to the corner or to their room every now and then, or ground them or take away privileges infrequently. But, there are few children who would not care if they knew that they would have to stay in their room or a guest room *every time* they talked back to you, even if it meant two or three days in a row. There are few children who would not care if they knew they would not be allowed to watch TV, talk on the telephone, or play *every day* that their homework was not completed. There are few children who would not care if they knew you would take their toys away *every time* that they left them around the house, even if it meant that you would do this day-in and day-out.

If you really care, the children will really care. If you are prepared to use all means necessary and appropriate to influence the children to eliminate their disruptive and inappropriate behavior, they will sense your determination and quickly care about the certain consequences that they will have to face if they choose to act inappropriately.

FAMILY EXAMPLE

In the previous chapters we have discussed how the parents, Emily and Steve, determined the behaviors and consequences of their Assertive Discipline Plan. Now we will discuss how the parents presented the plan to their children.

The morning after Emily and Steve had finished developing their Assertive Discipline Plan for each child, they sat down with the children as soon as they got up for school, before there were distractions. They firmly told Kevin and Karen how they expected them to behave.

> **Father:** Mom and I can not tolerate how you two have been behaving. We have had it with the constant hassles with the two of you. Kevin, you will do what you are told without arguing! Karen, you will do what you are told the first time, no excuses!

> **Mother:** I feel exactly as your father does. I've had it. Kevin, Karen, you will do what I tell you to do—the first time I tell you!

Father: Now if for any reason either of you choose to disobey what we have just told you, you will be disciplined. Here is the plan of what will happen. Kevin, let's start with you.

Mother (giving each child a copy of his or her Discipline Hierarchy): Kevin, the first time you do not cooperate, we will walk over and put your name on this chalkboard, which will be posted on the refrigerator. This will be a warning. The next time you do not cooperate we will put a check next to your name and you will be sent to your room for thirty minutes. When you are in your room, you cannot play with your games or listen to your tape player, and you will not get to watch TV for the rest of the day. If you do not cooperate again, we will put another check next to your name and you will stay in your room for an additional hour. If you do not cooperate a fourth time, you will receive another check, and you will be sent to your room for an additional hour and a half.

When we give you a check, we will not argue with you; we will not scream; we will not yell. We will send you to your room, and you are expected to stay there. If, for any reason, you come out before your time is up, you will go back, and we will add an additional half-hour to the time that you will have to stay in your room. If you play when you are in your room, we will take your games and cassette player out.

Every day we will start over fresh. That means each morning we will erase the chalkboard and give you a warning the first time you misbehave, just as we did the day before.

Father: Karen, basically the same thing will happen to you if you choose to misbehave, except that when you get one check, you go to your room for fifteen minutes without playing with your toys and lose TV, then two checks and thirty minutes, then three checks and one hour.

Kevin: Why do we have to have this plan?

Mother: We are setting up this plan because, as we said, we cannot tolerate your misbehavior.

Kevin: What if we do not like the plan?

Father: We can understand if you do not like the plan, but we are your parents and we feel that it is needed. Thus, the plan will go into effect immediately.

Kevin: How long will we have this plan?

Father: We will use this plan as long as it is necessary.

Kevin (getting angry): I think these plans are really stupid; they're not needed. There's no need for me to do all those silly things you ask me to do!

Mother: Kevin, you will follow my directions, and, if you do not, you will choose to go to your room. (*Broken record*)

Kevin: Sometimes I just don't want to do what you tell me to do!

Father: I understand, Kevin, but you will follow our directions the first time we give them or you will choose to be disciplined. (*Broken record*)

Kevin (folds his arms and shakes his head): All right, I hear you.

Father: We do not want to have to send either of you to your room, but if you act up and do not cooperate we have no choice. We care too much about you to allow you to act up as you have. We are your parents, and you have to listen to us whether you like it or not.

Mother (holding chalkboard): Now, to serve as a reminder for all of us, we will place your discipline plans right on the refrigerator. Next to them we will place this chalkboard that will be used to record your name and checks.

You can see that by following the guidelines we have presented, Emily and Steve were able to lay down the law in a clear, no-

nonsense manner to their children. They had taken the first step needed to reassert their authority and take charge of their children's misbehavior.

• In this chapter we have discussed laying down the law with your children. In summary, you and your spouse must firmly present your Assertive Discipline Plan to your children. Also, be prepared with a broken-record response if your children try to sidetrack you when you confront their misbehavior.

SOME QUESTIONS PARENTS ASK RELATED TO TOPICS IN THIS CHAPTER

Question: My twelve-year-old threatens to run away if I set up an Assertive Discipline Plan. How would you handle that?

Response: We have a question for you, who runs your house, you or your twelve-year-old? If you allow the threats of your children to deter you as a parent from dealing responsibly with your family, you are in trouble. You must let your child know that you, not she, decide what will happen in the household and that if she runs away, she will be dealt with firmly.

Question: Whenever I use the "broken record" on my son, he gets angry and yells at me to stop repeating myself. What should I do?

Response: Tell your son that if he does not like your using the "broken record" and repeating yourself, he should listen to you the first time you tell him something.

Question: Why is it that you repeatedly use grounding, or sending a child to his or her room, or taking away a privilege as disciplinary consequences?

Response: Sending a child to his or her room, grounding and taking away privileges are suggested frequently because, from our experience in working with parents, we have determined that these are consequences parents often use that work. We have found, however, that the key to dealing with your children's misbehavior is not what consequences you use but how you use them. Any consequence, when used consistently, will prove highly effective in motivating the vast majority of children to improve their behavior.

8

ASSERTIVE DISCIPLINE PLAN: STEP FIVE
Implementation

Moms and Dads, *please note:* Just laying down the law with your children may not improve their behavior one iota. You will need to establish consistently assertive responses to your children's behavior when they do, or do not, do what you want. You will need to be prepared to discipline your children every time they break your rules—no ifs, ands, or buts. No excuses. Break a rule—Go to your room, etc. without fail! Conversely, an equal amount of effort must be directed towards "catching your children being good." Your "I like that—good job" must permeate your interactions with your children minute by minute, hour by hour, day by day. Your children need to feel, "My parents care enough about me and my behavior to put in the time and effort necessary to insure I behave in a positive manner."

GUIDELINES FOR IMPLEMENTING THE PLAN

Here are some simple guidelines to follow to help you effectively implement your Assertive Discipline Plan with your children.

Provide the Consequence as Soon as Possible After the Child Chooses to Disregard Your Request.

When your children break your rules, immediately notify them of the disciplinary consequences. You may enforce the consequence at that time, for example by telling them, "You talked back; you chose to go to your room," or, "You did not do your chores; you thus chose to miss TV." On the other hand, you may inform the children of the consequence that will occur in the future: "You left home without permission; you chose to be grounded after school tomorrow," or, "You have been yelling and screaming in the car; you thus chose to go to your room as soon as we get back home."

Provide the Consequence in a Matter-of-Fact, Nonhostile Manner.

Many children get a real thrill out of getting their parents worked up into a frenzy. In such cases, it may be worth it to the child to be grounded, to miss TV, or to miss a privilege just to see you ranting and raving. To discipline children effectively, please be calm. Simply state, "You chose to have me . . . ," in a matter-of-fact tone of voice. You will communicate your message much more meaningfully if you are calm, cool, and collected. Let the children know you feel in control and communicate this through your voice and actions.

Never Take a Negative Consequence Away.

Many parents will reduce or rescind the disciplinary consequences they provide because their children have "improved" their behavior. One mother we worked with would take away TV privileges if her children misbehaved. Almost daily she had conflicts with her children before school and would tell them they they could not watch TV when they got home from school. Each day, her children would come home from school and would act like "angels." After about forty-five minutes of such "good" behavior, they would approach their mother, tell her they were "sorry for being bad" in the morning and ask for one more chance so that they could watch TV. Invariably the mother would give in. The next morning, the "game" would start anew. This mother could never understand why her children behaved so well in the afternoon, yet gave her fits every morning.

If your children choose to break a rule, they must be provided the consequences of their behavior. If you always back down and don't make your children serve out the consequences they have chosen, they will never learn that you truly mean business.

If Your Disciplinary Consequence Does Not Work, Change It.

Speaking realistically, some disciplinary consequences are not effective with some children no matter how consistently they are used. Some children would not mind missing TV, going to their room, or losing a privilege. If you have consistently utilized a disciplinary consequence and it is clear that your children's behavior has not improved, we recommend you do the following. Sit down and select a different consequence to utilize. Here is an example:

> **Parent:** Jeremy, I want you to stop making so much racket with your toys. We cannot hear the television with all the noise you are making. If you continue to make noise, I will have to take the toys away from you.
>
> **Jeremy:** O.K., Dad. (*After a few minutes he begins to fire his laser pistol, which makes a tremendous racket.*)
>
> **Parent:** Jeremy, that laser pistol makes too much noise. I have to take it away from you. Please give it to me.

Jeremy: O.K., Dad, here's the pistol. I'm sorry I made too much noise with it. (*Within ten minutes, Jeremy is playing with a motorized truck, which again distracts the entire family.*)

Parent: Jeremy, that truck makes too much noise. Now I told you I want you to stop playing with your toys and making so much noise. You have chosen that I take that truck. Now give me the truck. I want you to play with some quiet toys like your blocks.

Jeremy: (*Takes out his blocks and plays quietly for a couple of minutes, but then begins smashing them loudly.*)

Parent: Jeremy, stop making all that noise with those blocks. Give me those blocks now.

Even though his parents consistently followed through and took his toys away, Jeremy continued to make noise. It then became necessary for his parents to utilize a different consequence.

Parent: Jeremy, you have a choice: Either you play quietly in the family room with your toys, or you have to go outside and play.

Initially When Your Children Behave Reinforce Them Only with Praise.

Word of warning: It is not appropriate when you are attempting to lay down the law with your children to tell them you will provide them "goodies" if they behave. For the first day or two that you implement your Assertive Discipline Plan be sure to reinforce your children's appropriate behavior only with praise and no other rewards like those included in a Positive Contract or Marble Mania. Before such rewards are appropriate your children must know you are the boss and will firmly discipline them when they misbehave. Once you feel you are in charge, and your children know it and have improved their behavior, then it is time to further motivate them with various rewards.

If you are going to utilize a Positive Contract, Marble Mania, or any other rewards with your children, you will need to explain to them how and why they can earn such rewards. You may want to write down the positive rewards and post them next to the behaviors and consequences already on the chalkboard etc.

> Whenever Brian does his homework or chores he will get a point. When he earns ten points, he can have a friend sleep over.

> Whenever Seth and Lynda play cooperatively, they will earn a marble. When they have earned a hundred marbles they will get to go to McDonald's for lunch.

You Must Reinforce Your Children's Behavior Immediately.

In order to maximize the impact of your positive response, you should make the response as soon as possible after your children exhibit the behavior you desire. Too many parents praise their children at night for the behavior that occurred in the morning or let them go to the park because they behaved well earlier that week. Parents often make the mistake of offering long-range rewards to children. It is not fruitful to offer to a seven-year-old a new bike next summer for good behavior at school. Many parents promise their young children a special toy at Christmas for good behavior during the fall. Realistically, most children do not have the maturity or the mental capacity to hold long-range goals in mind day after day.

As soon as you observe or become aware of your children doing what you want, reinforce their behavior by letting them know, "I like how you . . ."

You Should Consistently Reinforce Your Children When They Behave.

When you begin to work with your children on improving their behavior, you will need to reinforce them: "I like . . . ," "Good job," etc., *every time* they engage in the behavior you have requested. Just praising or rewarding them once or twice will not produce results. You should be prepared to praise and reward your children consistently for several days, a week or two, or even longer, depending upon the child and his or her behavior, to get results. For example:

The parents praised their four-year-old daughter every time she got dressed by herself for one full week.

The parents praised their eight-year-old son every time he played cooperatively with his sister for nine days, and rewarded him at the end of this time by allowing him to pick his favorite restaurant when the family went out to eat.

The parents praised their twelve-year-old son every night that he did his homework for two weeks, and as a special reward gave him extra money to go skating at the end of this time.

Once you are comfortable with the fact that your children have shaped up and are consistently doing what you want, you can begin to gradually phase out your praise and positive support. Do not do it all at once. Do not go from praising your children every time they behave to praising them every fifth or sixth time they do what you want. If you cut your positive responses so dramatically, your children will just as quickly lose their motivation to behave, and you're back to square one.

When Your Children's Behavior Has Improved, Develop a New Assertive Discipline Plan for the Next Behavior You Want to Change.

As soon as you feel you have the initial misbehavior of your children under control, it is time, if there is another behavior you want to change, to move on to it. For example, a mother we worked with developed an Assertive Discipline Plan to help her get her son to come home on time. After a week of consistently following through, her son knew she meant business and came home when he was told to. The mother also had trouble getting her son to stop teasing his younger brother. So she sat down and developed a second Assertive Discipline Plan to help her deal more effectively with her son's teasing.

At this point you may be concerned that your children engage in so many misbehaviors that you will have to keep developing one Assertive Discipline Plan after another, seemingly forever. This will not be the case. From our experience working with countless numbers of parents, we have found that when you successfully lay down the law with one or two key misbehaviors, your children catch on that you mean business and realize they had better "shape up" in general. The comments of a fourteen-year-old son of parents we worked with sums this point up well.

He told us: "After my parents both let me have it about my mouthing off at them, I thought they were just on another one of their new kicks. But when they cracked down every time I got in trouble at school, I began to see they really were not kidding around. They are different. When they tell me to do something now I know they mean it. It does no good to argue or complain. I realize I had better stop all my messing around or my parents will sit down and start in again. Even though the last few weeks have been difficult, I do finally know what my parents expect of me and I realize what I can and cannot do."

If you follow the guidelines we have spelled out in this book for asserting yourself with your children, you can anticipate the same basic results with your children.

When Your Children's Behavior Is No Longer a Problem, You Should Eliminate the Use of Your Assertive Discipline Plan.

When you definitely feel your children will behave as you want them to, it's time to say goodbye to your Assertive Discipline Plan. Be sure your spouse agrees that the plan is no longer needed. Then, tell your children something like this:

"Your behavior has improved so much we no longer are going to use our Discipline Plan. We hope we never have to use a plan again. But if your misbehavior returns, we will not hesitate to do so. Finally, we really want to let you know how much we appreciate how you are behaving. Keep it up."

FAMILY EXAMPLE

In the previous chapter we discussed how the parents, Emily and Steve, presented their Assertive Discipline Plan to their children. We are now going to discuss the parents' experiences when they used their plan. Emily and Steve began to take charge immediately after presenting the plan. It took effort, for they realized they were paying the price for having been so lax in the past. They had never before responded so consistently. When one of their children began to argue or failed to do what he or she was told, the parents would firmly respond, "You were told to follow my directions. You chose not to, thus you will be warned, go to your room with no TV," etc. The parents made sure to keep track of their disciplinary efforts by keeping a record of each child's name and checks on the chalkboard on the refrigerator.

Concurrently, with their firm discipline, Emily and Steve made a concerted effort to praise the children when they behaved. As soon as their talk with the children was over Emily told them to get ready for school. When the children quickly complied, they were told by both their parents, "Kevin, Karen, we really like how you cooperated!" Praise was evident throughout the day. Both Emily and Steve stated they had never realized how necessary it was to balance their discipline with praise and positive support.

By the second day of using their plan, both Karen's and Kevin's behavior had improved dramatically. However, Emily and Steve, felt they should change Kevin's Discipline Hierarchy, removing the warning because Kevin did not care when his name was written on the chalkboard and responded only when he was sent to his room and lost TV. On one occasion on the second day he tried to sneak out of his room before his time was up. When Emily saw him, she told him, "That's half an hour longer for leaving your room early." Kevin began to loudly protest, "That's not fair!" Emily firmly responded, "You chose to leave your room early; you chose to get extra time."

By the end of the third day of using the plan, both the parents and the children noticed the change in the environment at home. Kevin told Karen, "Mom and Dad aren't kidding around. I think they are really serious about our behaving." Karen said, "I don't know about you, but I'm tired of spending time in my room."

Emily and Steve both felt they could finally get a handle on their children's behavior. Steve stated, "I feel the children will finally listen to me. I'm certainly more relaxed around them than I was a few days ago." Emily added, "I agree completely."

The parents believed they had begun to take charge and get control over their children's lack of cooperation. They thought it was a good time to introduce the marble rewards as a means to further motivate their children to improve their behavior. They sat down with their children again and the following dialogue ensued.

Mother: I'm really pleased with how both of you have improved how you follow directions.

Father: Let me tell you, I am pleased as well.

Mother: We have an idea to further let you know how much we like it when you do follow our directions. We have here a jar and marbles. Whenever one or both of you do what we want—that means you follow our directions the first time—we will put a marble in the jar. When you have earned seventy marbles, Kevin, Dad will take you to the video arcade and, Karen, you can have an extra dance lesson. Now if you both go all day without misbehaving and getting your name or a check on the refrigerator chalkboard, you will get a ten-marble bonus. Thus, the better you two behave, the quicker you will both get your reward.

Kevin (smiling): Now I know why you asked me all those questions the other day.

Karen: You mean all we have to do is be good and listen to you and we get marbles, and I get to take an extra class?

Father: Karen, that's right.

Kevin: How long will it take for us to earn the rewards?

Mother: That's up to you two. The more you cooperate, the more marbles you will earn and the quicker you will each get your reward.

Karen: When do we start?

Mother: Right now. Here is the jar and here are the marbles. I will place the jar right on the sink beside the refrigerator.

Emily and Steve found that it was much more difficult than they had expected to remember to consistently give the children marbles for behaving. At the end of the first day of implementing their reward plan, the children had only three marbles each in the jar. The parents decided to correct this problem by setting the timer on their oven to ring every hour or so in order to remind them to praise the children and to provide them marbles if they behaved.

By the morning of the fifth day the children's behavior had continued to improve. They both loved to earn marbles. Emily overheard Kevin telling Karen, "You know, if we listen to Mom, we can earn more marbles. Let's both be good so we can earn more." Karen replied, "You're right—I like earning marbles, but I really don't like going to my room."

That night Emily and Steve were going out and a sitter was staying with the children. Due to the recent problems Kevin and Karen had demonstrated when they stayed with sitters, the parents felt that it was necessary to assert themselves to make sure the children behaved.

When the sitter arrived they told the children in front of her, "Marie is the boss. Whatever she says, I want you to do. You will be in bed on time! We will call at your bedtime to be sure you have cooperated. If you do not cooperate with Marie you will get a 'check' and will stay in your room for the allotted time in the morning. If you do cooperate, you will earn a ten-marble bonus."

To say the least, the children were no problem for the sitter and were elated when the bonus marbles were dropped in the first thing in the morning.

As the children continued to cooperate without any problems, Emily and Steve felt it was time to move on to the next behavior they wanted to work on for each child. For Kevin it was doing his homework, and for Karen it was cleaning up after herself. The parents went through the same procedure as they did before and developed a new Assertive Discipline Plan.

The plan for Kevin was that he must do his homework correctly as soon as he got home from school. If he chose not to, he would not be allowed to go outside or play until it was completed. If he did do his homework as soon as he got home, he would earn praise and marbles.

Karen was expected to clean up after herself without being

told. If she did not, she could not watch TV or play until she did so. If she did clean up without being told, she would earn praise.

Emily and Steve firmly told the children what they wanted and again consistently followed through if the children did, or did not, comply.

Kevin, realizing his parents meant business by the way they had consistently handled his arguing, challenged them only once about doing his homework. Emily firmly responded to the challenge by telling him, "You will do your homework now. You will sit there at your desk and not go outside until it is done!" Kevin sat there for nearly an hour before he finally did it. That was enough for him, and he did not try to get out of doing his homework again.

Karen challenged her parents a few times—she hated cleaning up. Each time her parents observed her leaving a mess they told her she would not watch TV or play until it was cleaned up.

On the seventh day of using the plan, the children had earned seventy marbles, and that meant they got their rewards. By this time the tone of the family interaction had changed. The children had learned to be more cooperative and the parents were more consistent and positive. Kevin saw it from the children's perspective when he said, "Mom and Dad have changed. I didn't like it at first, but now I really know what I can and cannot do at home. There used to be a lot of yelling and screaming around here. It's really nice that it's gone." Finally, Mom summed it up: "I never thought it could be so calm around this house. This week was hard work, but worth it. I can never see having to go back to the stress and hassles of the past. It was just not good for any of us."

Postscript: After about a month the parents felt they no longer needed to utilize their Assertive Discipline Plans. They told the children their behavior had improved so much the plans were no longer needed and that they hoped they would never find it necessary to use them again.

• In this chapter we have discussed how to implement your Assertive Discipline Plan. The key points we want you to remember are: Follow through consistently when your children do, or do not do, what you want. When your children's behavior has improved you can develop an Assertive Discipline Plan for the next problem you want to work on. When you are in control, you no longer need to utilize an Assertive Plan.

SOME QUESTIONS PARENTS ASK RELATED TO TOPICS IN THIS CHAPTER

Question: You state that you must follow through with a disciplinary consequence every time a child breaks one of your rules. Yesterday my child broke one of my rules and I forgot to follow through. What do you suggest?

Response: Just because you did not follow through once does not mean all is lost. Being human, we all respond inconsistently at times to our children's behavior. We would recommend that you let your child know that you forgot to follow through but that you will not forget in the future.

Question: I am afraid that if I respond as consistently as you say, I would do nothing but discipline my children all day long. Is this so?

Response: You are not alone in your fear. Most parents feel as you do. To be honest, your fear and the fears of other parents are groundless. Your children may act up for a while, but when you set firm limits, they will soon recognize that you mean business and that there is nothing in it for them to continue misbehaving.

Question: My child often gets into trouble when he is at a neighbor's house, and I don't find out about it until several hours later. Is it still O.K. to discipline him when it is long after the behavior occurs?

Response: The key to providing the consequence is that you provide it immediately after *you* become aware of the behavior. Tell your child that "I just found out how you behaved" at the neighbor's house and then what is going to occur.

Question: I have tried to keep my son in his room, but he keeps coming out. I'm just not strong enough to make him stay. How can I use the ideas you present?

Response: A mother in a similar situation shared with us an excellent solution. She went next door and asked a good-sized male neighbor to assist her whenever necessary. She had the neighbor come over and together they sat down with her son and told him he would not be allowed to come out of his room. The neighbor said, "If you leave your room, your mom will call me, and I will be sure that you stay in your room." It is important to note that just the confrontation with the child was enough to stop him from challenging his mother. He realized his mother would not hesitate to call for help and that the neighbor was capable of getting him to stay in the room. By demonstrating her conviction to the child, she was able to regain control in this situation.

SPECIAL CONCERNS
RELATED
TO ASSERTIVE DISCIPLINE

9

ASKING FOR HELP
WITH DISCIPLINE PROBLEMS

Good discipline and teamwork are synonymous—you cannot have one without the other. In many households, though, one parent ends up with the weight of discipline on his or her shoulders. If this is the case in your family, there are ways to change it. In this chapter we will focus on how you can get the help you need to be a good disciplinarian.

At one of our recent Assertive Discipline workshops, the following interchange occurred. An extremely upset and frustrated mother blurted out, "I feel I am the only one at home who deals with the kids. I swear my husband is oblivious to the way those kids carry on. There are times they just act awful. When I discipline the children; he simply will not support me. He just says, 'Kids will be kids.' I can't take it." A husband chimed in, "My wife is the same way. She always wants to be 'nice' to the children, never wants to upset them. I always have to be the bad guy, and the children complain I'm picking on them. I feel just like you. I don't know what to do!" Both these parents are feeling the burden of trying to discipline their children single-handedly. They both need to *assert* themselves and get the help they deserve from their spouses.

The first step for those parents—or any parent in a similar situation—to get help is to recognize the fact that you, the parent, have the right to ask for it. When there are two parents in the house, those two parents must work together when dealing with the children. We know you are aware that your children test repeatedly to see if both you and your spouse mean what you say and say what you mean. If your children pick up from one of you that they have to follow your directions, yet sense that the other parent does not really care, the children will continue to misbehave. One parent can rarely get the children to behave without the active support of his or her spouse.

Let's look at how you can assert yourself with your spouse in order to get more support in dealing with the discipline problems of your children. Initially you will need to discriminate between the effective and ineffective responses you can make to him or her. To help you accomplish this, we again need to turn to the concept of assertive, nonassertive, and hostile responses.

When you respond in an assertive manner to your spouse, you will clearly and firmly communicate your wants and needs. From our work with families we have determined that a clear "I" message, "I want you to please help me with the children," is usually the most appropriate and effective response you can make. In most interactions it is not necessary to demand that your spouse support you, "You will help me with the children this minute, or else!" When you respond in an assertive manner to your spouse, you will in no uncertain terms let him or her know exactly what you want and need in relation to dealing with the behavior of your children. A direct response will maximize the possibility of your getting what you need in your interaction with him or her.

The effective, assertive response again needs to be compared to the ineffective, nonassertive, and hostile responses you can make to your spouse. When you respond in a nonassertive manner, you do not clearly or firmly state your wants or needs: "Why don't you try to do something with the kids?" This kind of nondirect response does not clearly or firmly communicate what you truly want your spouse to do. When you respond in a hostile manner, you respond in a way that criticizes or possibly degrades your spouse: "It's just disgusting how you let the kids act up and run all over you!" Such a response in all probability will provoke your spouse and will not help the two of you to work together.

To further help you discriminate between these assertive, nonassertive, and hostile responses here is an example of what we mean:

Phyllis was having problems trying to handle her teenage son, David. Her husband, Gil, worked long hours, and when he came home he did not want to be bothered with all her complaints regarding their son. Phyllis was near the end of her rope and wanted more help in disciplining David.

Phyllis initially approached her husband in a nonassertive manner, feeling she was a failure due to her inability to handle her son. All she ever said to her husband were indirect comments such as, "I'm having some problems again with David." Her husband would respond in his typically brusk manner, "Look, you're home with him. You do whatever you want. I'm sure it will be fine." Unfortunately, Phyllis did not pursue the conversation any further.

The problems with her son grew and so did her frustration and anger. Her anger eventually erupted, and one day she lashed out at her husband in a hostile manner, "I'm sick and tired of you never doing anything about our son's behavior. Why don't you get off your rear end and do something to the kid!" Those comments only made her husband defensive and provoked an argument.

After attending one of our workshops, Phyllis realized she must have help with her son and that there was nothing wrong with asking for it. She sat down with her husband and told him in a clear, assertive manner, "I have to have some help with David's behavior. I cannot handle him without more support from you!" Those comments were the beginning of a productive conversation about how her husband could help her deal with their son's behavior.

GUIDELINES FOR GETTING HELP FROM YOUR SPOUSE

In order to help you respond in an assertive manner to your spouse, we have developed the following guidelines for you to follow.

Plan How You Will Present Your Concerns to Your Spouse.

When you are in conflict with your spouse regarding his or her role in the discipline of your children, we have found that it is extremely useful to *plan* what you will say before you discuss the problem with him or her. Here is what we suggest you prepare before you talk with your spouse.

Decide upon goals for the discussion. What do you want from your spouse? In most instances you will want his or her cooperation and support in dealing with the discipline problems of your children.

> I need more cooperation from you, Dear, in dealing with the children.

What are your specific objectives? How do you specifically want your spouse to reach the aforementioned goals? In what ways do you want him or her to help out or change?

> "I want you to help me set up a discipline plan for the children." "I want you to discipline the children when they act up in front of you."

What is the rationale for the discussion? In the majority of discussions with your spouse, your reason for such talks will be as follows:

It is in our children's best interests that they know we are a team and that we will both deal with them when they do, or do not, behave.

State the consequences you feel will occur if your spouse does not offer the support you need. Be straightforward! Don't beat around the bush. Let your spouse know what you feel will occur if he or she does not give you the support you need with the children.

Unless you support me with the children, I feel I simply will not be able to get them to behave, and this house will become even more chaotic!

Unless you follow through on the Assertive Discipline Plan, I feel we will continue to have all of this tension in the house.

Unless you back me up in getting our child to behave, I think he will never learn to act appropriately.

When Appropriate, Utilize Assertive Communication Skills.

Some spouses have great difficulty discussing the discipline of their children. They may become hostile, evasive, defensive, or accusatory. If this is the case with your spouse, here are two assertive communication skills to help you get your point across as easily as possible. One of the techniques you are familiar with—the broken record; the other is new—we call it a "yes" or "no" response.

Broken Record:
This technique is, again, designed to help make your point and stick to it. To utilize this technique, you need to determine what you want from your interaction with your spouse. This should take

the form of a statement: "I need your cooperation in regard to our children's behavior," etc. In your interaction with your spouse, the broken record will be evidenced by the repeated expression of your message, thereby disregarding the "sidetracking" responses of your spouse.

> **Mother:** I need your cooperation to make sure the children do their chores and homework on the nights that I work late. (*Statement of want*)

> **Dad:** Look, I know I have to be more involved with the kids, but I'm beat when I get home. (*Sidetracking*)

> **Mother:** I understand, Dear, but you still need to make sure that they do their chores and their homework. (*Broken record*)

> **Dad:** You sure are persistent.

> **Mother:** You are right. The kids need to know it is just as important to you as it is to me that they do their chores and homework.

> **Dad:** I see your point. I will make sure they get everything done.

"Yes" or "No" Response

Your spouse may attempt to give vague responses when you request specific actions from him or her: "Well, I'll think about what you said," "What you said was interesting, I'll consider it," or, "I really want to do what you ask—I just don't know if it's possible." These responses are often attempts by your spouse to get you "off his [or her] back." The statement, "I'll think about what you said," may really mean, "Don't bother me anymore." If you do not pursue the issue, you will be left with no commitment—pro or con—from your spouse. It is necessary to assert yourself and determine where your spouse stands. This technique requires that you focus on any vague statement by your spouse and try to clarify what you feel your spouse is saying.

Father: We have to do something to make sure the children follow our Assertive Discipline Plan more closely. I feel we have to send them to their room every time they start acting up, just as we said we would.

Mother: Well, I don't know. It may be too hard on them. Let me think about it.

Father: I hear you saying you are not going to follow through as we said we would.

Mother: Not really. I just . . . ah . . . Oh well, I don't know.

Father: It is vital for our kids to know that we are working together. For their sakes, we can't wait any longer. We must be a team and follow through. I want to know where you stand—yes or no—can I count on you to follow through?

Mother: Well, yes, I will. You are right. You can count on me and my support.

The broken record and the yes and no response can help you to increase your confidence and ability to communicate more effectively to your spouse. Be sure to plan how you will use each of these techniques before you discuss the matter with your spouse.

Involve Your Spouse in Planning the Discipline Effort with Your Children.

The more you involve a reluctant spouse in determining your children's Assertive Discipline Plan, the higher probability you will have of getting his or her support. *Do not* sit down with your spouse and flatly state, "Here is what the kids have to do differently and here is how I want you to respond when they act up." Have your spouse provide ideas as to how to both discipline and reward the children.

To help you further understand the point we have just made on getting support from a reluctant spouse, here is an example of a parent utilizing these ideas.

Ethel and Roger both worked at careers. Many nights they did not get home until just before dinner. There were constant problems with the children, especially at this time, due to the children's "forgetting" to set the table, help fix dinner, and general disobedience. Roger did not like conflict, and whenever possible he would let Ethel handle the children. Ethel reached the point where she needed more support in handling the children, so she sat down with Roger and they had the following conversation.

Ethel: I am really fed up with the children. I feel I'm at them all the time and it does no good. Roger, I need your help in getting the children to behave. (*Goal*)

Roger: What's the problem now, Ethel?

Ethel: The kids don't help us get ready for dinner. They constantly argue with me and don't listen to a word I say.

Roger: You know, I think you just get too upset with those kids. Don't pay any attention to them.

Ethel: I understand your feelings, Roger, but I still need your help getting the kids to behave. (*Broken record*)

Roger: Well, what do you want me to do?

Ethel: I need your help in setting up a discipline plan, too . . .

Roger: What in the world is a discipline plan?

Ethel: In this book I just read, it states that it is helpful to set up rules for the kids to follow as well as consequences for behaving and misbehaving. I want you to help me set up the rules and the things we will do when they are good and when they are bad.

Roger: You usually discipline the kids. Why don't you just do it yourself?

Ethel: The kids must know we are working together, Roger, to make sure they behave. We cannot allow them to act as they do. We can't let them grow up acting like this. (*Rationale*)

Roger: Well, I think this discipline plan is going a little too far.

Ethel: I understand, Roger, but I need your support to get the kids to behave. I feel the plan is the best way to go. (*Broken record*)

Roger: You sure are serious about this, Dear, aren't you?

Ethel: You bet I am. The kids don't feel you are behind me, and that makes it impossible for me around here. Unless you give me more support, I've had it. You try handling the kids by yourself. Unless something is done, the stress will get to me! (*Consequences*)

Roger: I didn't realize it was so bad. Tell me what we need to start this discipline plan. I'll help you with it, and I'll let the kids know they must shape up!

Please note: If your spouse is not very cooperative in relation to disciplining the children, it may prove helpful to ask him or her to read this book. Your spouse may thus gain a better understanding of how you arrived at your ideas and, in addition, may be more willing to accept the ideas from so-called experts, rather than from his or her spouse.

One last point: If your spouse has become an ex-spouse, it may be much more difficult to get his or her support in dealing with the children. It will be even more important to follow the ideas we have just presented in this chapter.

• In this chapter we have discussed how to ask your spouse for help. Here are the points we want you to remember: You have a right to ask your spouse for help in dealing with your children's misbehavior. In order to maximize the effectiveness of your communication with your spouse you should respond in an assertive manner. Finally, you should plan what you are going to say to your spouse before you meet.

SOME QUESTIONS PARENTS ASK RELATED TO TOPICS IN THIS CHAPTER

Question: I am having a great deal of trouble handling my children. Their bad behavior is truly driving me up the wall. My husband, though, is not comfortable being firm with the kids. He just doesn't want hassles. What am I to do?

Response: As we stated, you will have to assert yourself with your spouse. You must clearly and firmly let him know you will not tolerate the way your children act. Express the fact that you have needs just as the children do. Let him know you are going to assert yourself with them and that you definitely want and need his support.

Question: I am divorced and my ex-husband constantly tells our children that I am too hard on them and that they really don't need to listen to me. What do you suggest?

Response: Obviously, you need to tell your ex-husband that what he is saying to the children is not in their best interests. If you cannot get him to stop making statements like that to your children, it will be necessary for you to sit down with your children and tell them very clearly that no matter what their father says, when they are with you, you are the boss and they are going to have to follow your rules.

Question: My husband thinks it's "cute" the way our daughter always acts up in public. She has to be the center of attention whenever we go out. I can't stand the way she acts. What do you suggest?

Response: Tell your husband exactly how you feel. Let him know that you are not comfortable with how your daughter acts and that it is definitely not in your daughter's best interest to have to be the center of attention whenever you go out.

10

BUT WHAT IF THEY DON'T BEHAVE at SCHOOL?
The Use of Assertive Discipline with School Behavior Problems

We are well aware that many of your children have had problems behaving at school as well as at home. In this chapter we will spell out in detail how you can work with your children's teachers and principal in order to prevent problems from developing and to eliminate them if they occur. First, some background information pertaining to the behavior problems in today's schools is necessary.

DISCIPLINE PROBLEMS IN TODAY'S SCHOOLS

Disruptive student behavior is the number one problem facing our nation's schools. Children are no longer the passive and obedient students that we typically were when we went to school. The hundreds of thousands of educators with whom we have worked report to us that at the present time between 15 and 30 percent of students at any given school engage in some form of problem behavior requiring special attention from their teacher or principal.

Why is this so? There is no simple answer. A number of complex factors combine to create this problem. We addressed this issue in our book, *Assertive Discipline: A Take Charge Approach for Today's Educators.* In this volume we wrote:

The role status of the contemporary teacher, as with any authority figure in society, be it law officer, doctor or even President, has declined in recent years. Up until a few years ago, the teacher was viewed in "awe" by both students and their parents. The teacher, simply because of her role status, had respect and authority. Thus, she was a very "powerful" figure in the eyes of the students and could easily influence the students' behavior, often with just a look, a smile, or a threat.

All of that is now changed, more, of course, in some areas than in others. Today, a teacher has to *earn* the respect of both students and their parents. Children, especially in the upper grades, do not hold their teacher in the "awe" they used to. Often, a teacher's look, smile, or threat is simply disregarded by such students. In reality, the teacher's basic techniques of influence (discipline) are no longer as effective in getting the desired results. The discipline approaches of the 1950s and 1960s do not work with the students of the 1970s.

In addition, the teacher cannot rely upon the unending support of all the students' parents. Many parents are openly questioning, sometimes with justification, the education that their children are receiving, and do not feel they want to support the wants or needs of their child's teachers.

The changes in the students' and parents' perceptions of the role status of teachers have been paralleled by changes in how teachers view themselves. It is no longer fashionable to be the "rigid, authoritarian, traditional, disciplinarian" of bygone days. Instead, psychology, namely the philosophies of Doctors Freud, Skinner (Behavior Modification), Glasser (*Schools Without Failure*), and Gordon (*P.E.T* and *Teacher Effectiveness Training*) has been brought into the classroom. These philosophies of discipline have had a major impact upon contemporary teachers. The problem is that these ideas have often been *distorted* and misinterpreted to the point that teachers have been led to believe fallacies such as:

If you discipline a child you will cause him irreparable "psychic trauma."

Avoid all conflict with the child. If a child is "ripping apart" the classroom, don't confront him, find him an alternative activity that will better meet his needs.

Teachers *must* understand the causes of a child's problem behavior. The child may be driven by "unconscious" drives and cannot control his "neurotic" behavior.

Finally, even though the average teacher may be called upon to teach in each class three or more students with behavior problems, he or she has had *no* formal competency-based training in how to deal with such students. It may be hard to believe, but from our experience less than 5 percent of our nation's teachers receive training in their college courses in handling discipline problems.

The various factors of lowered teacher role status, lack of parental support, philosophical conflicts, increasing number of disruptive students, and lack of teacher training all have contributed to the critical discipline problem in today's schools.

As we stated in the Introduction, in response to this problem we developed our program Assertive Discipline for Educators, in the late 1970s.

GUIDELINES FOR STUDENT BEHAVIOR

In the Assertive Discipline for Educators program, we espouse the same basic principles of dealing assertively with children that we have discussed in this book from the standpoint of parents. The teacher must be the "boss" in the classroom. No student has the right to be so disruptive that the teacher cannot teach or other students cannot learn. We emphasize again the reality that all children have the right to be with adults who care enough about them to put in the *planning* necessary to enable them to set firm, consistent limits when the children get out of hand and who, at the same time, realize the children's need for warmth and positive support.

In order to utilize Assertive Discipline, teachers are instructed to do the following:

Establish the rules they need to teach in their classrooms. A typical set of rules for an elementary classroom might be:

1. Follow directions.
2. Raise your hand and wait to be called on before you speak.
3. Keep your hands, feet, and objects to yourself.
4. Stay in your seat unless you have permission to leave it.
5. No cussing or teasing.

A typical set of rules for a junior or senior high school classroom might be:

1. Follow directions.
2. Swearing or making obscene gestures is not allowed.
3. Leaving the classroom is not permitted without a proper hall pass.
4. You must be in your assigned seat with all necessary materials when the tardy bell rings.
5. No food, candy, or gum shall be eaten during class.

Establish a set of disciplinary consequences that students will receive if they choose to break the class rules. Here is an example of a typical "discipline plan" a teacher might utilize.

First disruption	Student's name on board
Second disruption	One check, fifteen minutes after school
Third disruption	Two checks, thirty minutes after school

| Fourth disruption | Three checks, thirty minutes after school and call parents |
| Fifth disruption | Four checks, thirty minutes after school, call parents, send to principal |

Establish a plan to reinforce students when they do behave. The plan should include consistent praise, positive notes to parents, and rewards if the entire class behaves.

Establish a plan to work very closely with parents. Teachers should let the parents know about their classroom discipline efforts by sending the parents a copy of their discipline plans. On page 156 is a typical letter a teacher may send home to parents describing their Assertive Discipline classroom plan.

In addition to the use of Assertive Discipline in the classroom, principals are encouraged to set up rules, disciplinary consequences, and positive consequences to help ensure that students behave in the halls, cafeteria, on the yard and field. Here is an example of the typical "Schoolwide" Assertive Discipline plan.

A Typical School Discipline Plan

We at Johnson School believe the students can behave. We feel that all students have a responsibility to behave in a manner that prevents neither teachers from teaching, students from learning, nor violates the best interest of any individual in the school community. In order to encourage our beliefs, the following school discipline plan has been established to govern behavior at school.

Out-of-class behavior rules for the halls, cafeteria, yard:

1. Follow directions.
2. Stay in designated areas.

Dear Parent:

In order to guarantee your child, and all the students in my classroom, the excellent learning climate they deserve, I am utilizing the following Discipline Plan starting today.

My Philosophy:

I believe all my students can behave appropriately in my classroom. I will tolerate no student stopping me from teaching and/or any student from learning.

My Class Rules

1. Follow directions.
2. No shouting out.
3. Get work done on time.
4. Be to class on time.
5. Clean up your own mess.

If a Student Chooses to Break a Rule

1st consequence Name on board.

2nd consequence 15 minute detention.

3rd consequence 30 minute detention.

4th consequence Call to parents.

5th consequence Go to principal's office.

Severe disruption Go to principal's office.

Students Who Behave Will Earn

Praise

Positive notes and awards

Extra free time

It is your child's best interest that we work together in relationship to his/her schooling. I will thus be in close contact with you regarding your child's progress in my classroom. Please sign the tear-off and have your child bring it with him/her to school tomorrow. If you have any questions or comments, please feel free to call me or write them on the tear-off.

Sincerely yours,

_____

Teacher signature

Dear

I read and understood the Discipline Plan for your classroom.

_____

Parent/guardian signature

3. No littering on campus or in the halls.
4. No fighting.
5. Use equipment properly.

Disciplinary consequences for breaking rules:

First offense	Benched remainder of period
Second offense	Benched and parents called
Third offense	Benched, parents called and five days with no noon activities
Fourth offense	Benched and parent conference

Positive consequences for behaving:

Positive consequences will be provided to students who behave. Students who do not break a rule for a quarter-semester will be invited to attend a special awards assembly.

If your children's teachers are using Assertive Discipline, you may be familiar with the principles we have just presented. The overwhelming number of parents whose children's teachers and principals utilize Assertive Discipline are one hundred percent behind the program because it enables teachers to get back to teaching and students to get back to learning.

WORKING WITH YOUR CHILDREN'S SCHOOL

Our Assertive Discipline program is not a "cure-all," enabling teachers to get all students to shape up. In addition, only about one-fourth of the nation's teachers are utilizing any or all aspects of Assertive Discipline in their classrooms, and to tell the truth, some use it more effectively than others. Thus, your children may still be having behavior problems at school. If this is so, here are pointers on how you can work with your children's teachers and principals to eliminate those problems.

We want to begin by sharing with you some important, down-to-earth facts to be aware of when working with your children's teachers.

Teachers don't like to call parents and tell them they are having a problem with their children. Teachers have been told that they should be able to handle all behavior problems on their own with no help from parents. This is nonsense; yet many teachers and principals still hold to this misguided belief. As a result, teachers usually put off calling you until the problem with your children has become serious. In addition, they will tend to downplay the problem they are having in order not to look bad or upset you. For example, teachers typically say, "We are having a *small* problem with your child's attitude," etc. Don't be misled. If a teacher or principal contacts you, there is a problem that needs to be dealt with, and your help is definitely required.

Because teachers are reluctant to admit they can't handle their students, it is not uncommon for a child to have had problems for several years and their teachers not to have contacted his or her parents. Thus, when out of the blue your child's teacher calls and explains the problem he or she is having with your child, you may feel (especially after listening to your child) that the teacher is picking on your child or that there is a personality conflict between them. The reality is that in all probability the teacher is a skilled professional who is concerned enough about your child to work with you to help the child.

There are several reasons why your children's teachers must have your cooperation in helping your children to shape up. First, as we have noted, your children's teachers just do not have the "clout" our teachers did. When our teachers told us to "do it," we responded, "How quickly?" Today's students may respond with a blasé "I don't feel like doing it," or a flat-out "No!" Your children must know you are one hundred percent behind their teachers and that you will go to any means necessary to support them. Second, you obviously know your children better than their teachers know them. You know best what your children would dislike happening to them if they act up and, on the other hand, what could be used as motivation to reward them if they do behave. Finally, don't overlook the fact we presented earlier—the average teacher has not been trained to handle behavior problems. Teachers were trained to teach reading, writing, arithmetic, science, history, etc. They were not taught how to deal with the disruptive behavior in which today's children engage.

Now let us turn our attention to the specific details of how to work successfully with your children's teacher or principal.

Determine the Specific Problems Your Child is Having at School.

When your child's teacher, principal, or counselor contacts you regarding problems they are having with the child at school, determine the exact nature of the problem. Do not settle for, "He's been bad," or, "She has to change her attitude." Ask questions: What does my child do wrong? When does he or she do it? How often does it occur? Why does it occur? Ask for any documentation of the problem: for example, incompleted work, the school's discipline records. Through your questioning, you will want to achieve a clear picture of the nature and severity of your child's problems.

It will be useful to determine also what the teacher or principal has done in the past in response to your child's misbehavior. What type of discipline have they utilized? What type of reinforcement have they utilized? What approaches have worked? What approaches have not worked? This information will help serve as a baseline upon which to build future responses to your child's behavior at school. To further illustrate how to work with your child's school we will follow the example of a concerned parent we worked with.

Mrs. Lewis received a call from her son Brian's sixth-grade teacher, Ms. Kerry, regarding his constant problems at school. In the course of the conversation, Brian's mother came to understand that, rather than do his work in class, he would act silly and disrupt the children around him. Ms. Kerry reported that she had tried taking away his recess and free-time privileges when he acted up and praising him when he behaved, but this simply was not working.

Determine a School-Home Assertive Discipline Plan for Your Child.

Teamwork between home and school is necessary if you want your child to improve his or her behavior. You and your child's teacher—and possibly vice-principal, principal, or counselor—will want to set up an School-Home Assertive Discipline Plan for guidelines on how you will all respond to your child's behavior. The School-Home Assertive Discipline Plan is similar to an Assertive Discipline Plan. It will (1) specify the behavior you want your child to follow at school and (2) detail how the teacher and if necessary the principal will respond when your child does, or does not, behave. The plan will also (3) include your responses when you receive feedback about your child's school behavior. In other words, the School-Home Assertive Discipline Plan is designed so that, depending upon how your child behaves, he or she will be disciplined or rewarded both at school and at home.

Whenever possible, we recommend that you go to school and meet with your child's teacher and principal. Face-to-face contact is advantageous when you are dealing with such serious problems as those related to your child's misbehavior at school.

In your discussions with your child's teacher and principal, you will need to determine what they specifically expect from your child and what negative and positive consequences they will provide your child for his or her behavior. In most instances, especially if the teacher is using Assertive Discipline, he or she will already have this information available and may have previously shared it with you.

If your child's teacher does not have a plan, we would strongly recommend that you suggest the need to set one up with your child. (See Appendix for worksheet.)

Your child's misbehavior may occur outside of the classroom—in the halls, on the playing field, or in the cafeteria—and the school principal or vice-principal may be the one responsible for dealing with your child. If this is the case, ascertain the plan of action the principal or vice-principal has decided to utilize with your child.

Once you understand how the school will deal with your child, determine what assistance you can give. In most instances, it will be beneficial if you back up the school by rewarding or disciplining the child at home, depending upon the "good" or "bad" report that you receive from the school.

Finally, your efforts with the school must be based upon solid day-by-day monitoring of your child's behavior by telephone or, more commonly, by note. Each day, the teacher or principal will need to send you a note indicating how your child behaved and how you should follow through at home. Conversely, each morning you will need to send the teacher a note indicating your efforts at home. Let's go back to our example of Mrs. Lewis and her son Brian.

Brian's mother went to school and met with Ms. Kerry. They agreed that it was in Brian's best interest that they set up a School–Home Assertive Discipline Plan to help him.

Ms. Kerry determined the following rules Brian must follow in class: Do what I tell you to do. Do your work. Do not talk or disrupt the children sitting next to you.

She decided that if Brian broke a rule, she would utilize these consequences:

The first time he broke a rule: His name would be put on the board.

The second time he broke a rule: Twenty minutes sitting alone in the back of the class.

The third time he broke a rule: Forty minutes sitting alone in the back of the class.

The fourth time he broke a rule: He would be sent to the principal's office to do his work.

Ms. Kerry decided that when Brian did behave he would earn a star, and when he earned ten stars he would receive a Positive Citizen Award, which was the big reward that all the children in class wanted.

The mother and the teacher further agreed that Mrs. Lewis should follow through at home. Every day Ms. Kerry would send a note home with Brian indicating how he had behaved that day in class. If he had not completed his work, the assignment would accompany the note, and his mother would see that he finished it at home. If the note indicated that Brian had misbehaved, his mother would not allow him to watch TV that night. If the note indicated that he had behaved, she would give him a point, and when he had earned five points, she would take him to buy a fish for his aquarium.

Sit Down with Your Child and Share the School-Home Assertive Discipline Plan.

Once you and the school staff have determined your plan of action, we would strongly recommend that you, the teacher, and any other school personnel involved, sit down face-to-face with your child and, as a group, "lay down the law." Your child must know that he or she has to behave at school and that both home and school are working together to help motivate the child to shape up.

The child should be presented the specifics of the School-Home Assertive Discipline Plan. The child must know the behaviors he or she must engage in; what the school staff will do if the child does, or does not, behave; and how you will follow through at home.

When Brian's mother and teacher had completed their plan, they sat down with Brian and clearly asserted their demands.

Ms. Kerry: Brian, you will do your work in my class—without disrupting!

Mrs. Lewis: Brian, I will not tolerate your behavior at school. You will do whatever your teacher tells you.

Brian: You don't understand. It's not my fault . . .

Mrs. Lewis (interrupting): That's not the point. You will do what Ms. Kerry says!

They then proceeded to tell Brian what they both would do if he did, or did not, behave in class. His mother concluded the conversation by stating:

Brian, you are very fortunate to have a teacher like Ms. Kerry who cares so much about you. I will not see you fail at school. We are going to work together to help you, and you will improve your behavior.

Make Sure You and the School Follow Through on the Plan.

Keep on top of the implementation of your School-Home Assertive Discipline Plan. Follow through each night at home, rewarding or disciplining your child in accordance with the feedback you receive from school. Monitor the school's efforts. Is the teacher sending you home a note every day? Does the note indicate what you are to do? Is the teacher disciplining your child in class if the child misbehaves? Is the teacher reinforcing your child in class if the child behaves? Is the principal or vice-principal following through, if necessary?

If your child's teacher is doing a good job, here's a helpful hint—let the teacher know how much you appreciate his or her efforts. Today's teacher does not get enough strokes for doing his or her job. In addition, either call or send the principal a note explaining what a fine job your child's teacher has done.

Dear Mr. Shannon,

I just want to take this opportunity to let you know of my sincere appreciation for the job Ms. Kerry has done with my son Brian. She has gone to great effort to make sure that we can work together to help Brian behave at school. It is a pleasure working with her.

Sincerely yours,
Elizabeth Lewis

If, on the other hand, your child's teacher is not following through and working with you as planned, be sure to call him or her and determine why. If you are not satisfied with the response, it may be appropriate to ask the teacher to arrange a meeting with you and the principal to discuss the matter further.

It is important to be aware that the vast majority of teachers are excellent professionals. There are, though, a small percentage of teachers who, for various reasons—frustration, "burn-out," incompetence—do not put forth the effort necessary to deal effectively with children and parents. If this is the case, we repeat: It is in your best interest and your child's best interest that, after talking with the teacher, you arrange a meeting with the principal to resolve the matter. Back to our example of Mrs. Lewis and Brian.

Each day in class, Ms. Kerry closely monitored Brian's behavior. Misbehavior resulted in his being sent to do his work alone in the back of the class, while appropriate behavior was greeted with, "Good work, Brian. Here's another star." Each afternoon, his mother read the note from the teacher and responded accordingly at home.

Dear Mrs. Lewis,

Today Brian's behavior was unacceptable. He disrupted twice in class and did not finish his math. It would be helpful if you made sure he finishes his math and, as we discussed, take away TV privileges because of his disrupting in class.

Thank you,

Ms. Kerry

A note like this indicating he had not behaved was responded to with a firm, "Finish your work in your room, and no TV."

Dear Mrs. Lewis,

Today Brian's behavior was excellent. He did all of his work and did not disrupt once. It would be helpful if you rewarded him by giving him another point toward earning his reward.

Thank you,

Ms. Kerry

A note like this indicating he had behaved was responded to with "Good job at school. Here's a point toward earning your fish."

Each morning Brian's mother sent his teacher an appropriate responding note.

Dear Ms. Kerry,

I received your note about my child Brian's misbehavior at school. Last night I made sure he finished his math and he was forbidden to watch TV.

Sincerely yours,

Mrs. Lewis

or,

Dear Ms. Kerry,

I received your note about my child Brian's behaving excellently at school. Last night I gave him another point toward his reward.

Thank you.

Mrs. Lewis

Within one week Brian had begun to improve his behavior. He had earned two Positive Citizen Awards and one tropical fish.

Within two weeks his mother and his teacher decided to cut the notes down from daily to weekly because Brian had turned his behavior around and was doing his work without any problems.

When your child's behavior has improved, you will want to phase out the notes from daily to weekly and then, when appropriate, stop them. We would suggest, though, that you still periodically call your child's teacher or principal to make sure your child is behaving in an appropriate manner.

We have one last point for this chapter. The key to your children's behavior at school is your involvement and support of the teachers' efforts with them. Too many of today's parents have the attitude that "my children are the school's responsibility from 9:00 to 3:00." Your children must know that you, in no uncertain terms, will not tolerate their misbehavior at school. Your children must know that you consider their teacher as the boss in the classroom and they are to do whatever he or she says. In conclusion, your children must know you expect them to behave at school—no ifs, ands, or buts!

• In this chapter we have discussed how to deal with your children's misbehavior at school. Your children's teachers and principal must have your help in dealing with your children's behavior at school. You should set up a School–Home Assertive Discipline Plan to help structure your efforts with your children. Finally, always remember that your children must know you will not tolerate their misbehavior at school.

SOME QUESTIONS PARENTS ASK RELATED TO TOPICS IN THIS CHAPTER

Question: My son says it's not fair that I discipline him at home for his misbehavior at school because he was disciplined by his teacher for the behavior. What do you have to say to this?

Response: Let your child know it would be even less fair for you not to discipline him at home for his misbehavior. Let him know that you and the school are working together as a team to make sure he behaves in a manner that is in his best interest at school.

Question: I set up a behavior contract with my child's teacher, but she had not followed through on the plan. She says she's too busy to send notes home every day about how my child misbehaves. What can I do?

Response: First, I would contact the teacher and let her know that you want to know each day how your child behaves at school. If that does not work, I would go to the principal and tell him or her that you need more support from the teacher in order to deal with your child's inappropriate behavior at school.

Question: My child always says the other kids in class act up so much that they cause him to get worked up and misbehave. What do you have to say to this?

Response: Inform your child that he is responsible for his own behavior. Let him know that no other child can make him act up in class. He, not the other children, is in control of his actions, and you will accept no excuses for his misbehavior at school.

Question: My child got a terrible report card because of his misbehavior. I had no idea there were any problems at school. What do you suggest?

Response: I would demand a meeting with your child's teacher. I would let the teacher know I was extremely unhappy that I had not been informed earlier about my child's problems. I would want to establish a plan of action with that teacher to help my child improve his behavior at school. If I did not get satisfaction from the teacher, I would immediately go to the principal and share my concerns. As a parent, you have the right to know how your child behaves at school, and there is no reason for a teacher's not informing you!

Question: My child is always getting into trouble at school due to his fighting. He says the other kids provoke him. What do you suggest?

Response: I would firmly let my child know that I would not tolerate his fighting at school for any reason. I would want to talk to him about alternative behavior he can engage in other than fighting with the children when he is provoked.

Question: Isn't it really more effective just to allow the school to handle my children's problems that occur there?

Response: Absolutely not! Too many parents believe that the child's behavior at school is the school's responsibility to handle. As we stated before, your children must know that you and the school are both working together.

Question: My daughter was bad at school, and the teacher kept her afterwards. As a result, she missed the bus, and I had to come to get her. I was very put out about it. What can I do about this?

Response: If you did not like having to pick up your child at school, we would recommend that you tell your child to listen to the teacher so that she will not be disciplined. If your child's behavior is such that she must be kept after school for disciplinary reasons, it should be a clear message to you to let your child know she had better improve her behavior at school.

Question: My son behaves fine at home, but he is real problem at school. Could it be the school's fault?

Response: It is possible that the teacher is not handling your child correctly. It is more probable that your child simply does not behave at school. Just because your child, in your opinion, behaves at home, it does not necessarily follow that he behaves in other situations—including school. In all too many cases today, parents tend to blame schools for their child's problems. We would recommend that you sit down with your child's teacher and principal, hear what they have to say, and take their comments very seriously.

Question: My teenager is a severe behavior problem at school. He is often tardy, and when he does get to class he is very disruptive. We have tried everything with him, including disciplining him at home and suspending him from school. Do you have any ideas?

Response: When you have tried everything else with a child who is such a problem at school, there is one approach you may want to attempt. With the approval of the school, you or your spouse may want to attend your child's classes and monitor his behavior for the entire day. A mother we worked with did this and reported the following. "My son was constantly in trouble at school. Both the school personnel and I got fed up, so I decided to spend an entire day with him at school. I made sure he got to class and I sat in the back of each class to to make sure he behaved. My son hated this, to say the least. He reported to me at the end of the day, 'I never want this to happen again.' I told him I felt the same way. Ever since that time he has behaved. I didn't like doing it, but it produced results when all else had failed." Using the same technique when all else has failed may get results for you as well.

11

ASSERTIVE DISCIPLINE
ADDS UP TO CARING

Throughout our discussion of Assertive Discipline we have presented numerous concepts and techniques: taking charge and being the
boss, consistency, Assertive Discipline Plan, broken record, positive
contracts. The cornerstone of these concepts—indeed, the cornerstone of the entire Assertive Discipline approach—adds up to one
word, CARING. No concept or technique we have presented will
benefit you or your children unless you care enough to put in the
time and effort needed to use these concepts in a manner that will
ensure that your children behave. If you do care enough to do what
must be done you can get results. This point is of great significance,
and we need to elaborate upon it.

WAYS TO SHOW YOUR CHILDREN THAT YOU CARE

There are several key ways you can demonstrate to your children
that you do truly care about how they behave. First, you can anticipate situations in which your children may have trouble behaving
and help your children deal with them before they occur. Next,
you can exert the time and effort necessary to develop and use the
Assertive Discipline Plan whenever your children's misbehavior

demands its use. Finally, you can demonstrate your sincere determination that your children behave by putting forth the effort whenever necessary to see that they do. Let's discuss each of these important points.

Anticipate Problem Situations Before They Occur.

One way you can demonstrate your concern for your children's behavior is to anticipate problem situations before they occur and help your children deal with them. For example, your children often have problems when they go to restaurants, go to Grandma's house, or play with certain children. Before any one of these situations arises you would want to sit down with your children and tell them, "You have had problems behaving in this situation in the past and I cannot allow you to misbehave again. If you choose to misbehave, I am prepared to discipline you." Here is an example that will illustrate what we mean.

Carol was a divorcee who frequently had severe problems with her children when they returned from weekend visits with their father. Their father did not discipline the children and they came back "high as a kite." It typically took her a full day or two of screaming at them before her children would listen to her. Carol realized this pattern was not good for her or her children and she needed to do something.

When her children arrived home the following Sunday night, the first thing she did after she greeted them was to sit down with them and say, "I know it's hard for you to have Mom and Dad divorced. I know you are excited when you come home from staying with Dad. But I cannot tolerate the way you two usually behave the first few days after you return. You cannot act so wild—you have to listen to me! I care too much about the two of you to let you act so disrespectfully. Now, I expect you to behave and, if either of you chooses not to, I am prepared to take away TV and ground you."

By anticipating problem situations, you are letting your children know you are on top of their behavior, and that will more than likely prevent uncomfortable situations from recurring.

Utilize an Assertive Discipline Plan When New Problems Develop.

Another way you can demonstrate your concern is by putting forth the effort to develop Assertive Discipline Plans when new problems develop. Many parents use an Assertive Discipline Plan for one or two problems, and, after those problems are resolved, fail to use the approach in the future. They revert to less effective approaches, which often result in the same conflicts as in the past arising between them and their children. The answer is for you to utilize an Assertive Discipline Plan whenever your children's misbehavior calls for it. Here's what we mean:

> Mel and Kathy were bewildered by how to get their children to stop teasing and fighting with each other. The parents had tried everything, and they finally reverted to screaming and threatening the children. Finally and successfully the parents utilized an Assertive Discipline Plan to handle the problem. A few months later the eldest son began to get into trouble fighting with the children in the neighborhood. As before, the parents found themselves screaming and threatening their child in an attempt to get him to behave.
>
> After a few weeks of conflict with their son, Mel stated to Kathy, "I've had it with this yelling and screaming. What we need to do is make up a plan to help us deal with our son's misbehavior." Mel and Kathy did just that and were soon able to once again help their son improve his behavior.

Always keep in mind that an Assertive Discipline Plan is a tool to enable you to help your children stop their misbehavior.

Put Forth the Effort to Ensure Your Children Know You Mean Business.

There may be times you need to demonstrate your concern for how your children behave by truly inconveniencing yourself. This may mean, for example, your children's behavior demands that, rather than going out, you stay home and make sure they do their homework; having returned home from a night out, you must discipline your children after you speak with the sitter and find out they misbehaved; or you monitor your children's behavior when you would much rather be relaxing and watching TV. Here's a further example of what we mean.

Jim and Betty were confronted by their teenage son's constant problems at school. He was in trouble almost daily. The school staff had tried everything they could and were at the point of wanting to suspend him if he got into trouble again. Jim and Betty realized that they had to cooperate more closely with the school, but they both worked and it was extremely difficult for either of them to take time off. After a lengthy discussion, both Jim and Betty realized they would have to inconvenience themselves to help their child. Because Jim's schedule was more flexible than his wife's he arranged with his boss to take time off and meet with his son's principal and counselor. At this meeting it was agreed that the next time Jerry was a problem he would be suspended and one of the parents would pick him up from school, grounding him in his room for as long as his suspension lasted.

The following week Jerry was suspended for the remainder of the school day and the following day. Betty arranged to leave work, pick him up, and make sure he stayed in his room. Jim arranged to stay home the following day.

Jerry knew how hard it was for his parents to take time off from work and was shocked that each of them did so. He told his principal, "I can't believe my folks stayed home. I guess they really are serious about making sure I behave here." Jerry's behavior at school improved immensely after his parents demonstrated their concern to him.

When you assertively take charge with your children and show your concern by anticipating problems, utilizing an Assertive Discipline Plan when necessary, and being willing to put forth the effort to ensure they behave, you are telling them that you do care about how they behave.

By assuming an assertive take-charge attitude, you are saying, "I care about my family. It is my responsibility to firmly guide my children's behavior in a direction that is in their best interests as well as the best interests of others, including myself."

One mother summed up this point very well when she said to us, "Look, I realize the buck stops with me and my husband in our home. If we don't make our children behave, who will? There are times that I may not like all this responsibility, but this may sound corny, I love my kids too much to stand by and let them act up the way some parents do."

When you, the parent, care about your children and demonstrate your caring by assertively taking charge, your children will benefit, you will benefit, your family will benefit.

IV

APPENDIXES

Appendix 1

DISCIPLINARY AND POSITIVE CONSEQUENCES

In this appendix we will list resource ideas which can serve as the consequences to be utilized when your children do, or do not, behave. All the consequences presented have been successfully utilized by parents. We want to emphasize a vital point: You must be comfortable using any consequence, positive or negative, that you choose. *Please do not take any idea we present and use it unless you and your spouse both feel it is appropriate for your family.*

We will begin with disciplinary consequences which you may find useful. The first consequences we present are those designed to be used with minor behavior problems. They will be followed by those designed to be used with serious behavior problems.

We define minor behavior problems as "annoying," run-of-the-mill misbehavior most children engage in from time to time. These problems can cover a wide range: "forgetting" to follow directions, "hassling" you when it is time to get ready for school or at bedtime, sibling rivalry, not doing chores, periodic attention-getting outbursts, or minor problems related to school.

We define serious behavior problems as those that severely challenge parental authority, are dangerous, self-destructive, or threaten the well-being of the family unit. Also, if your children engage in a number of minor problems, their behavior should be considered serious.

Please note: None of the disciplinary consequences listed will be effective unless they are used in a consistent manner.

DISCIPLINARY CONSEQUENCES FOR MINOR BEHAVIOR PROBLEMS

Let's discuss the specific disciplinary consequences that you could find useful with minor behavior problems. Many of them, in all probability, are consequences that you have already used with your own children, but there are a few that may be new and prove useful to you. Again, use only those consequences you feel are appropriate for your family!

Separation

When the child is disruptive or will not cooperate, the child is separated from you and others into a nonstimulating, "boring" situation: standing in a corner, sitting in his or her room. The child should initially be given approximately the number of minutes of separation equal to his or her age: for example, a six-year-old should be given six minutes. If possible, use a kitchen timer to monitor the amount of time to be served. Tell your child, "You will stay in your room [or in the corner] until the bell goes off." The timer will help handle the yells of "When can I come out?" and prevent a parent, under some circumstances, from forgetting the child. If your child creates a disturbance while being separated, add more time. "Whenever you jump around while you are in the corner, you will stay another minute." Separation is a useful disciplinary consequence for children from ages approximately two to eleven.

Examples
Separate a three-year-old in the corner for three minutes for refusing to leave you alone while you were on the phone.

Separate a five-year-old in his or her room for five minutes for arguing with you.

Separate a seven-year-old for seven minutes for grabbing his brother's toys.

Word of warning: Some children will not stay in their rooms when placed there. Make sure you keep the child in his or her room and that you add more time if he or she leaves. You may want to remove games, toys, radio, TV, stereo, etc., from the room, so the child will not have entertainment.

Comment: Separation is probably one of the best disciplinary consequences to use with pre-school and school-age children. Children "hate" not being part of the action. It is a gentle, yet highly effect consequence.

Taking Away Privileges

Taking away privileges includes suspending the right to watch TV, eat snacks, play with toys, participate in sports, use the telephone, or stay up late. Parents usually suspend privileges by degrees: no TV for one night, then two nights, then all week. Whenever possible, the privilege taken away should relate to the nature of the problem. You forbid TV-watching because your child watched TV instead of doing homework. You take away use of the telephone because your teenager spoke longer than was allowed.

Examples

You take away for one week your eleven-year-old son's right to have friends over because he and his friend made a mess in the back yard.

You take away your seven-year-old's bike for one week because he rode it into the street.

You take away snacks from your ten-year-old daughter because she ate doughnuts five minutes before dinner.

Word of warning: Be careful not to deny privileges for too short or too long a period of time. It's best to start with a short period of time—just one day—and build if the problem continues.

Comment: Taking away privileges can be an effective disciplinary consequence at all age levels from pre-school on.

Physical Actions

Actions speak louder than words! The most appropriate response to your child's misbehavior may simply be to go up to him or her and physically accomplish what you want.

Examples

You take the ashtray away from your toddler when he does not comply with your request to put it down.

You go to your eleven-year-old's room to turn down the stereo when she does not comply with your request to do so.

You take your four-year-old by the arm and make him clean up his toys when he refuses to do so.

You escort your six-year-old to the dinner table when she does not come when called.

You take the toy gun away from your eight-year-old when he will not stop firing it in the living room.

Word of warning: Do not use excessive force when moving your child. The goal is to back up your words with action, not to hurt or frighten the child. Be sure to give him or her a choice: "Go to your room or you choose to have me take you there." Finally, physical action is most appropriate with younger children, typically those up to the age of ten.

"Do What I Want First."

Doing what you have asked first is a common-sense approach to management that all parents use. You tell the child that until he or she has complied with your request, the child cannot do something that he or she desires: "You cannot eat dinner until you wash your hands," or, "You cannot go outside until your room is cleaned."

Examples

Your children cannot watch TV or go outside until their homework is finished.

Your eight-year-old cannot have a snack until his chores are finished.

Children cannot eat breakfast until they are dressed and their beds are made.

Word of warning: Stick to your word. If you say that there will be no breakfast until the child is dressed, be prepared for the child to miss breakfast.

Comment: This is a mild consequence that works for all age levels.

Grounding

You restrict your child to his or her room, house, or yard. The length of the restriction and the severity are related to the severity of the problem behavior.

Examples

Yard grounding: The child is restricted to the house and back yard for one day because he went into the street without permission.

House grounding: The child is grounded in the house for

two days for lying to you about where he went after school.

Word of warning: Don't overuse grounding—maximum, one week for house or yard. Also, grounding will not work for children who don't care to be out and around the neighborhood.

Comment: Grounding is a highly effective consequence for school-age children, including adolescents, if used consistently.

THE MOST COMMON MINOR PROBLEMS AND HOW TO HANDLE THEM

Here are some typical minor problems parents encounter. We have provided you with examples of consequences that you may find useful with each problem.

PROBLEM	DISCIPLINARY CONSEQUENCE
Your seven-year-old goes away from home without telling you.	You ground the child at home for the following two days.
Your nine-year-old disrupts and argues at the dinner table.	Your child finishes his dinner alone in his room.
Your children argue and fight over which TV program to watch.	Neither child is allowed to watch TV for the remainder of the evening.
Your six-year-old rides her bike into the street.	You take her bike away for three days.
Your four-year-old makes a mess in the family room with her toys and will not clean them up.	You clean up the toys and do not give them back to the child for three days.
Your eleven-year-old will not pick up the dirty clothes.	You clean up the dirty clothes and take the clothes away for one week.
Your thirteen-year-old and his friends mess up the living room.	They are not allowed to go into the living room.

Your four-year-old acts up at the market.	She is sent to her room as soon as you return home.
Your six-year-old acts up at a restaurant.	He is sent to his room as soon as you return home.
Your ten-year-old continually sneaks sweets between meals.	The child is not allowed in the kitchen by himself.
Your three-year-old keeps whining and complaining.	The child is sent to the corner for several minutes.
Your four-year-old continually interrupts you when you are on the phone.	The child is made to stand in the corner away from you until you are off the phone.
Your three-year-old has a tantrum when she does not get her way.	She is carried to her room and left there until she calms down.
Your children argue and fight.	Each is sent to a separate room for an appropriate amount of time.
Your teenager constantly ties up the phone.	You take away the phone privileges for the following day.
Your teenager stays out after curfew.	She is grounded for one week.
Your eight-year-old does not do his required chores after school.	The chores must be done as soon as the child comes home from school, and until they are finished, the child cannot play outside, watch TV, or have a snack.
Your eight-year-old will not take a shower.	His shower must be taken after dinner, and until it is, he cannot play or watch TV.
Your eleven-year-old will not clean his room.	The child must have his room cleaned Saturday morning or he is not allowed to leave his room that day.
Your six-year-old will not eat the food you serve her at dinner.	She cannot leave the table to play or watch TV until the food is eaten.

| Your twelve-year-old will not do his work at school. | His schoolwork must be finished at home before he is allowed to play or watch TV after school. |
| Your teenager will not do her homework. | Her homework must be finished before she is allowed to talk on the telephone. |

DISCIPLINARY CONSEQUENCES FOR SERIOUS BEHAVIOR PROBLEMS

Now let's discuss some specific disciplinary consequences you could find useful with serious problems. You may find that some of the consequences previously mentioned for use with minor problems are also appropriate for use with serious problems. Again, use only those consequences you feel would be appropriate for your family!

"I Am Watching You."

"Watching" is an extremely close monitoring of the children's actions. It may even include violating the children's privacy. This is necessary when the children have engaged in behavior of a serious nature outside of your supervision. The consequences are most effective when you tell the children, "I am going to be watching you." You may want to tell the children how you will be watching: "I am going to come to your classroom to make sure you are behaving," but not what day you will be doing so.

Examples

You tape-record your children after they have been severely disruptive with sitters and listen to the tape to determine who was acting up. You may also utilize the tape recorder at school if the children have been a problem in class.

You require your teenager to provide you with sales slips for all purchases after he was caught shoplifting.

You walk into your child's classroom unannounced (teacher and principal know) after becoming aware he has been refusing to cooperate with the teacher.

Word of warning: These consequences should be used only in severe situations. Children, especially teenagers, do not like their privacy being violated. Be sure to tell the children that you will "snoop" unless they choose to improve their behavior.

Comment: For some children, such methods are necessary to let them know you care about them and that you really do mean business.

Outside Help

There are times when you may want or need assistance from other adults in disciplining your children. They may include your spouse or ex-spouse, the teacher, principal, the local law-enforcement authorities, or a trained counselor or therapist.

Examples

Your son is extremely disruptive and will not listen to you, so you tell him you will call his father at work and have his father come home to deal with him.

Your daughter will not listen to you, so you have your ex-husband talk with her.

You cannot get your daughter to do her homework, so you have her teacher make her finish it during free time at school.

You are unsuccessful in getting your child to behave, so the family seeks family counseling.

Word of warning: Outside help should be sought only when you have attempted all other means available to you. Whenever possible, it is best for the adult involved in the conflict with the children to handle it on his or her own.

Comment: In this day and age, with so many one-parent families, it is not uncommon for the parent to need outside assistance. Counseling, in particular, can be an invaluable aid in improving your relationship with your children.

Room Grounding

Room grounding is the most severe form of grounding. Your children are basically isolated in their rooms with *no* TV, stereo, telephone, games or toys. The children are allowed to leave the room only to attend school, go to the bathroom, and to eat.

Examples

You room-ground your twelve-year-old for one day for cussing at you.

You room-ground your teenager for two days for sneaking out without permission.

You room-ground your eleven-year-old for two days for hitting and kicking his younger brother.

Word of warning: Don't overdo room grounding—a maximum of one or two days at a time is sufficient.

Comment: Room grounding is called for when children are a highly disruptive influence in the family. It should only be utilized after less severe consequences have been attempted.

Out-of-Home Grounding

When children are flagrantly disruptive and blatantly noncooperative, they are sent to be "grounded" for a few hours or days with a neighbor or a relative. These individuals must be cooperative and agree not to make the stay "fun." The children should be required to stay in the neighbor's or relative's house without TV, stereo, or toys. If the stay is to be for an extended period of time, the children should be allowed to leave only to go to school and come back.

Examples

Your ten-year-old is highly disruptive and will not stay grounded, so you make him spend the remainder of the day grounded at your neighbor's.

Your teenager will not listen to you or respond to your limits, so you have him grounded for two days with your ex-spouse.

Your teenager cusses and strikes you, so you have him grounded for two days with his aunt and uncle.

Word of warning: This is obviously a severe consequence and should always be a last resort. Use only with older children and adolescents.

Comment: Out-of-home grounding could have a dramatic impact with many children. Sending a child away can break a cycle of conflict that has developed over a long period of time between parent and child.

SERIOUS PROBLEM BEHAVIORS AND HOW TO HANDLE THEM

Here are some examples of serious problems that parents encounter and consequences that parents have found useful in dealing with them.

PROBLEM	DISCIPLINARY CONSEQUENCE
Your teenage daughter continuously lies to you about where she is going.	You ground her in her room for two days.
Your eleven-year-old does failing work at school.	You forbid TV and sports until his grades improve.
Your ten-year-old disrupts the family dinner by angrily provoking his younger brother.	He finishes his meal in his bedroom.
Your twelve-year-old vandalizes a wall at school.	You make him clean it up and pay for damages out of his allowance.
Your eight-year-old is suspended from school.	He is made to stay in his room without TV or toys the entire time he is suspended.
Your twelve-year-old simply will not listen to you.	You arrange out-of-home grounding at the neighbor's for the remainder of the day.
Your seven-year-old willfully smashes his sister's toys.	He is made to pay for the toys out of his allowance.
Your teenage daughter's friends smoke marijuana at your house while your are away.	She is grounded and not allowed to have friends over again when you are not home, for three months.
Your ten-year-old steals money from your wallet.	She is made to repay you with her allowance and is grounded.
Your ten-year-old maliciously and continuously provokes his brother and sister while watching TV.	He loses the right to be in the family room and watch TV for one week.

POSITIVE CONSEQUENCES

We will now discuss the positive consequences you can utilize in your Assertive Discipline Plan when your children do behave. Before we discuss positive consequences you will first need to decide which of your children's behaviors you will want to reinforce. We will list typical problem behaviors your children may engage in and the appropriate behavior that you desire and will want to reinforce.

PROBLEM	DESIRED BEHAVIOR
Child leaves home without telling you.	Child asks permission to leave.
Child argues at the dinner table.	Child eats quietly.
Child argues and fights over which TV program to watch.	Child cooperates with other family members.
Child rides bike in the street.	Child rides bike where you ask.
Child does not clean up toys.	Child cleans up toys.
Child leaves dirty clothes out.	Child cleans up clothes.
Child whines and complains in market.	Child is cooperative.
Child acts up at restaurant.	Child eats and behaves appropriately.
Child sneaks snacks between meals.	Child does not eat without permission.
Child constantly whines and complains.	Child talks in appropriate tone of voice.
Child continuously interrupts you.	Child is quiet when you are talking.
Child has tantrums when he does not get his way.	Child cooperates and follows your directions.
Child does not get ready for bed.	Child gets ready for bed.
Child stays out after curfew.	Child comes home on time.

Child lies.	Child tells the truth.
Child goes to bed screaming and yelling.	Child goes to bed quietly.
Child argues and complains.	Child cooperates.
Child constantly demands attention.	Child plays by himself.

EFFECTIVE POSITIVE CONSEQUENCES FOR TYPICAL BEHAVIOR PROBLEMS

Here are examples of effective ways that you can back up your words with action when your children do behave.

PROBLEM BEHAVIOR	MOTIVATOR FOR BEHAVING
Your nine-year-old disrupts and argues at the dinner table.	He is allowed to choose dessert if he behaves.
Your children argue and fight over which TV program to watch.	The children are provided extra TV time if they cooperate.
Your six-year-old rides her bike into the street.	She is allowed to stay out later if she stays on the sidewalk.
Your four-year-old makes a mess in the family room with her toys and does not clean them up.	She is given a jelly bean every time she cleans up.
Your eleven-year-old will not pick up his dirty clothes.	He earns an allowance for picking up his clothes.
Your four-year-old acts up in the market.	You allow him to choose a treat if he cooperates.
Your six-year-old acts up at the restaurant.	He is allowed to choose a dessert if he behaves cooperatively.

Your four-year-old continually interrupts you when you are on the phone.

You give her a happy-face sticker when she does not interrupt you.

Your three-year-old constantly whines and complains.

You provide her a few peanuts every time she talks to you in an appropriate voice.

Your three-year-old has tantrums when he does not get his way.

You provide him extra time with you when he cooperates.

Your four-year-old keeps getting out of bed.

You give him a happy-face sticker for staying in bed.

Your four-year-old will not share her toys.

You give her a few mints when she does share her toys.

Your five-year-old will not get ready for bed on time.

You read him a story when he does get ready for bed on time.

Your three-year-old becomes hysterical whenever you leave.

He gets a treat from the sitter if he does not cry.

Your four-year-old goes to bed every night crying and screaming.

She will earn special time with you in the morning if she goes to bed quietly.

Your five-year-old will not play by herself. She constantly follows you around.

You will let her earn extra time with you for story-reading when she plays by herself.

Your five-year-old continually comes into your room in the middle of the night.

He will earn a 10 cent toy plane each night that he sleeps in his room without coming out.

Your teenager continually lies to you about where she is going.

Every time you check with her and she has told you the truth, she has earned a point. When she has earned ten points, she may attend a party.

Your eleven-year-old does failing work at school.

Every day that his work is done at school, he will earn a point. When he has earned ten points, he may get his bike painted.

Your ten-year-old disrupts the family by angrily provoking his younger brother.	Every day that he does not provoke his brother, he will earn a point. When he earns five points, he will be allowed to go to a movie.
Your eight-year-old is suspended from school.	Every day that he behaves at school, he will earn a point. When he earns ten points, he may go fishing with his father.
Your twelve-year-old does not listen to you.	Every time that he cooperates, he will earn a point. When he earns one hundred points, he will get a bonus on his allowance.
Your eleven-year-old continually lies to you.	Every day that he does not lie, he will earn a point. When he has earned fifteen points, he may go to the car races.
Your nine-year-old is very disruptive whenever the family is together.	He will earn a point for every hour that he is quiet and cooperative. When he has earned thirty points, he may go to the toy store and buy a small toy.
Your six-year-old cries and screams and does not want to go to school.	You put a surprise treat in his lunch box each day that he goes to school without getting upset.
Your five-year-old constantly complains about physical ailments that are not real.	You provide her special time for playing with her favorite toy each day that she does not complain.

Appendix 2

ASSERTIVE DISCIPLINE
PLAN WORKSHEETS

The following worksheets are designed to help you set up and implement your Assertive Discipline Plan.

Step One of Your Assertive Discipline Plan: Determining Specific Behavior Your Children Must Change.

List all the specific behaviors you and your spouse would like your children to change.

Child's Name _____   Child's Name _____

1. _____   1. _____
2. _____   2. _____
3. _____   3. _____
4. _____   4. _____
5. _____   5. _____
6. _____   6. _____
7. _____   7. _____
8. _____   8. _____

Which specific behaviors do you and your spouse feel your children *MUST* change?

Child's Name _____   Child's Name _____

1st _____   1st _____

2nd _____   2nd _____

3rd _____   3rd _____

4th _____   4th _____

Start working on one, or maximum two, behaviors per child.

Step Two of Your Assertive Discipline Plan: Determining the Disciplinary Consequences You Will Use If Your Children Do Not Behave.

After reviewing the consequences presented and discussing the issue with your spouse, what consequences will you use with your children's misbehavior? Fill out the following questionnaire.

Child's Name _____

Behavior _____

The Disciplinary Consequence You Will Use:

Separation ____
For How Long? _____

Take Away Privilege ____
Which? _____

Physical Action ____
Which? _____

ASSERTIVE DISCIPLINE PLAN WORKSHEETS

Do What I Want First ____
What Will You Prevent Child From Doing? _____

_____

Grounding ____
   Yard ____
   For How Long? _____

   House ____
   For How Long? _____

   Room ____
   For How Long? _____

   Out Of Home ____
   With Whom? _____
   For How Long? _____

"I Am Watching You" ____
How Will You Monitor? _____

Outside Help ____
Who? _____

Other ____

_____

What will you do if this consequence does not work?

_____

What consequence will you then use?

_____

What will you do if your child simply will not comply with your disciplinary consequence: e.g., will not stay in his or her room?

_____

If you are using a Discipline Hierarchy, what consequence(s) will you provide your child?

The 1st time he/she misbehaves _____

_____

The 2nd time he/she misbe- haves _____

_____

The 3rd time he/she misbehaves _____

_____

The 4th time he/she misbehaves _____

_____

If your child misbehaves when you are not present, how will you monitor the problem behavior?

Telephone ____

Neighbor Visit ____

Who? _____

Tape Record ____

Written Note _____

Step Three of Your Assertive Discipline Plan: Determine How You Will Reinforce Your Children If They Do Behave.

If you are not sure what rewards would most motivate your children, sit down with them, one at a time, and ask them the following questions:

What do you like to do best with mother?

_____

ASSERTIVE DISCIPLINE PLAN WORKSHEETS

What do you like to do best with father?

_____

Who would you like to spend more time with?

_____

Suggestions:

Mother   Uncle

Father   Friend

Grandmother   Other

What would you like to do more often at home?

_____

Suggestions:

Have friends over   Use parents' tools, tape player,

Pick TV programs   etc.

Stay up later   Rent video movies

Select food for dinner   Play special games

Play sports   Do arts and crafts projects

Have party   Do hobbies

                                Other

Where would you like to go more often?_____

Suggestions:

Park   Fishing

Movie   Camping

Swimming   Horseback riding

Video arcade   Sleep at friend's home

Favorite restaurant   Shopping

Library   Toy store

Hiking   Sports event

                                Other

What food would you like to have more often?

_____

If you had more money, what would you buy?

_____

Suggestions:

Toys	Records or tapes
Games	Arts and crafts supplies
Books	Hobby supplies: models, coins,
Food	stamps
Makeup	Jewelry
Sports equipment	Camping equipment
	Clothes
	Other

Which reward of those we have just discussed would you most want to earn?

_____

Next:

What appropriate behavior(s) will you reinforce?

_____

_____

What positive rewards are you and your spouse comfortable using?

Extra time with you or spouse ____

Doing what with child? _____

Extra time with other family member or relative ____

Doing what with child? _____

Special activity ____

What, where, when? _____

Special food ____

What kind? _____

Material reward ____

ASSERTIVE DISCIPLINE PLAN WORKSHEETS

What, how much, when? _____

Other ____

_____

_____

Do you plan to use a positive contract? If so:
What behavior(s) do you want your child to engage in?

_____

What will you provide your child when he/she behaves? E.g, point,
star.

_____

How many points, stars, etc., will it take to earn the reward?

_____

What reward will the child earn?

_____

Do you plan to use a marble plan? If so:
What reward(s) will the children earn?

_____

_____

How many marbles will they have to earn to get the reward?

_____

Step Four of Your Assertive Discipline Plan: Laying Down the Law.

Fill out this worksheet before you meet with your child.

_____ I want you to _____
Child's name   Behavior(s) to change

If you choose not to do what we told you, we will

_____ .

Disciplinary consequence

If you are using Discipline Hierarchy, present consequence for:

1st time (you do not do what   _____

         you were told)   _____

2nd time   _____

                       _____

3rd time   _____

                       _____

4th time   _____

                       _____

How do you feel your child may try to manipulate you?

       "You're picking on me" _____

       Belligerence _____

       "I'm sorry" _____

       Crying _____

       "I hate you" _____

       Other _____

Remember: Use a broken-record response if appropriate. Present your positive consequence only when your children's behavior has improved.

Asking for Help

Before you meet with your spouse, fill out this worksheet.

ASSERTIVE DISCIPLINE PLAN WORKSHEETS

Goal for conversation (I need your help with the children, etc.)

_____

_____

What do you specifically want your spouse to do?

_____

_____

_____

Rationale for why you are talking to spouse.

_____

_____

_____

Consequences you feel will occur if he/she does not help you.

_____

_____

_____

School-Home Assertive Discipline Plan

If your child is having problems behaving in class, have his/her teacher(s) fill out this form.

What rules do you want my child to obey in your classroom?
1. _____
2. _____
3. _____
4. _____
5. _____

What will you do the first time my child breaks one of your rules?

_____

What will you do the second time my child breaks one of your rules?_____

What will you do the third time my child breaks one of your rules?

_____

What will you do the fourth time my child breaks one of your rules?_____

What will you do the fifth time my child breaks one of your rules?

_____

What will you do when my child follows your rules?

_____

If your child is having problems behaving outside of class in the school, the halls, yard, etc., have the principal, vice-principal, counselor, etc., fill out this form.

What rules do you want my child to obey in the halls, on the yard, etc.?
1. _____
2. _____
3. _____
4. _____
5. _____

What will you do the first time my child breaks one of your rules?

_____

What will you do the second time my child breaks one of your rules?_____

What will you do the third time my child breaks one of your rules?

_____

ASSERTIVE DISCIPLINE PLAN WORKSHEETS

What will you do the fourth time my child breaks one of your rules?_____

What will you do the fifth time my child breaks one of your rules?

_____

What will you do when my child follows your rules?

_____

How do your child's teacher(s), principal, etc., want you to support their efforts?

_____

_____

How will you monitor your child's behavior at school?
Note _____ Phone Call _____ Other _____

What disciplinary consequences will you provide your child if he/she misbehaves at school?

_____

What positive consequence will you provide your child if he/she behaves at school?

_____